Best Hikes With
CHILDREN®
San Francisco's
North Bay

Bill McMillon
with Kevin McMillon

THE
MOUNTAINEERS

To Kim and Derrick.
May you enjoy hiking as much as I have.

0 9 8 7 6
5 4 3 2

Published by The Mountaineers
1001 SW Klickitat Way, Seattle, Washington 98134

Published simultaneously in Canada by Douglas & McIntyre, Ltd., 1615 Venables Street, Vancouver, B.C. V5L 2H1
Published simultaneously in Great Britain by Cordee, 3a DeMontfort Street, Leicester, England, LE1 7HD

Manufactured in the United States of America

Edited by Lorretta Palagi
Maps by Evelyn Phillips
Cover photograph and all other photographs by Bill McMillon
Cover design by Elizabeth Watson
Layout by Bridget Culligan Design

Library of Congress Cataloging in Publication Data
McMillon, Bill, 1942-
Best hikes with children: San Francisco's North Bay / by Bill McMillon with Kevin McMillon.
p. cm.
Includes index.
ISBN 0-89886-276-0
1. Hiking—California—San Francisco Bay Area—Guidebooks.   2. Family recreation—California—San Francisco Bay Area—Guidebooks.   3. San Francisco Bay Area (Calif.)—Description and travel—Guidebooks.   I. McMillon, Kevin, 1982– .   II. Title.
GV199.42.C22S26948   1992
917.94'6—dc20   91-45547
                                                                                CIP

Contents

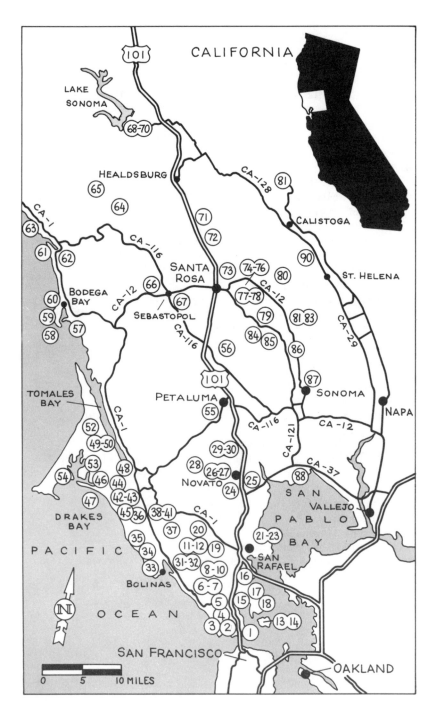

Introduction

One of my great pleasures is hiking along a fog-shrouded ridge or through a somber and solemn redwood forest with my wife and son Kevin. Fortunately, as a San Francisco Bay Area resident, I am blessed with a wide variety of such places to hike. There are trails throughout the region for all ages and physical abilities, and they provide everyone an access to nature that is lacking in the city and its suburbs.

From the open grasslands of the Marin Headlands to panoramic views from atop Mount St. Helena, this guide describes dayhikes in the North Bay that I have enjoyed in the past two decades, and that you can explore with your family, from young children to grandparents. Some are short hikes of less than one-half mile, suitable for even the youngest and oldest in your group, while others are more than five miles long for those who want both to enjoy nature and engage in pleasurable, vigorous physical activity.

HIKING WITH CHILDREN

Some children can't resist stopping to wade along a slow-moving stream, or watch an acorn woodpecker drill holes in a pine tree. Others want to push on up a trail to reach a hidden beach or an exposed mountain peak as quickly as possible. Each enjoys hikes in his or her own special way, and does so with great bursts of enthusiasm. And parents find such enthusiasm contagious.

Even the most enthusiastic child sometimes needs a little added encouragement to make it through a day's hike, however, and the following guidelines can help you get through those times—making hikes fun for all.

Know Your Family's Preferences

Each family has its own ideas about hiking. While some decide on a destination and concentrate on reaching it, others are more spontaneous, and reaching a particular destination is of only secondary importance. The same is true for members within a family. Some like to surge ahead along the trail to a rest stop where they may dawdle for a while; others like to take a more leisurely pace along the trail with shorter rest stops.

After an outing or two, you will know what your family prefers, and you can plan future trips with those preferences in mind.

Plan a Destination

Talk about your destination before you begin hiking, and let everyone know what is to be seen and explored along the way. Find a creek, a particularly interesting tree, or an outstanding vista, and plan to stop there. You may not make all the planned stops, but your family will have markers to help measure their progress during the hike.

You don't have to be intimately familiar with a trail to do this, because you can find information in this guide, or from other sources, to help plan a hike.

Plan for Nourishment and Rest

Always carry plenty of water, or other liquids, and snacks—even on short hikes. These can be used as incentives when the trail gets steep, or the day gets warm, and your charges begin dragging. A simple reminder that "We will stop at the next shady spot to have some water and energy food" will give all the impetus to continue along the trail.

Also, remember to take plenty of "energy" stops so no one on the hike gets overly tired.

"Adopt" a Child for the Day

You may want to bring a friend or friends along on the hike so each child has a companion with whom to share discoveries and rest stops.

Accentuate the Positive

Praise, such as "You certainly did a good job coming up that hill," is important to children, and it lets them know that you are aware of how much effort they are putting into an activity.

If a child shows signs of slowing down on a difficult section of a trail, distractions and patience, i.e., casually observing some trailside plants or rocks as your child overtakes you, or a "Look at that soaring hawk," will help with progress along a trail.

Tired Children

While most parents have a good idea of how far their children can hike, and plan their outings with those limitations in mind, there are times when the best laid plans go awry.

There are ways to overcome what are seemingly insurmountable problems, though. In the mid-1970s my wife and I took our four-year-old son on a camping trip to Point Reyes National Seashore with a group of high-school students. All went well until the last day of the trip when we discovered that we had neglected to study thoroughly a topographical map of the area. The first portion of the trail from Wildcat Canyon to Bear Valley was a rugged climb. One that no four-year-old could make without help.

Even with the assistance of several teenagers who carried one of our packs and most of our supplies, we began the day with trepidation. The first half-hour went fine, but drastic measures were soon needed. First, I carried Matt piggyback, but there was obviously a limit to this. He needed some incentive to walk more, and that incentive turned out to be a game of hide-and-seek.

Mary and I used our snack supply and took turns heading up the trail to hide a goody behind a rock or plant. We then encouraged Matt to scurry up the trail to find them. A successful search was followed by a short energy break while the snack was eaten.

This game got us over the hump, literally, and we made it to our car in a reasonable time. We learned a valuable lesson, however, and ever since we choose hikes that take in the abilities of *everyone in the family*, checking out the entire trail on a topographic map if we haven't hiked it before.

Of the many ways to avoid such problems on dayhikes, the best is to develop contingency plans for turning back short of your original destination. To help you with your hike plans, I have included "turnaround" sites for longer one-way hikes, and the "point-of-no-return" for longer loop hikes where it will be shorter to continue than to go back.

Have Fun Along the Way

Hikes should be fun. Enjoy yourself and help others enjoy themselves. Explore the area along the trail, and experience the sights, sounds, and smells of nature as you move along the trail. Remember, your goal isn't necessarily to reach a specific destination, but to have an enjoyable outing with your family where your children learn to enjoy and respect their natural environment.

TRAIL ETIQUETTE

Regardless of how well you plan a hike or how well behaved your children are, there are times when things don't go right. And there are certain rules of behavior that are expected of all hikers, whether they are children or adults.

The Call of Nature

All the suggestions of "go to the bathroom now, there isn't one on the trail" won't prevent an occasional crisis when your child has to go, and go immediately. If the child merely has to urinate, take him or her at least 200 feet from any trail or creek. If your child must defecate, dig a hole at least six inches deep in which to bury the feces. The used toilet paper (and you should always carry a small roll) should be wrapped in a plastic bag and carried out for proper disposal.

Uncontrolled Children

Hiking should be fun, but uncontrolled children who run rapidly around blind trail curves, yell loudly, and destroy plants and wildlife aren't fun for anyone. Always set ground rules for your children and any friends brought along on a hike.

Talking about these rules well beforehand lets everyone develop a positive approach toward how to act in the wilderness. Rather than just talking about what not to do, help your children see what others do that is undesirable, and emphasize that "good hikers" don't do those things. By the time you get on the trail they will be on the lookout for such negative behavior and will need little encouragement to avoid it themselves.

One rule that is frequently violated by children is cutting across switchbacks. Children love to slip and slide down a hill as they run ahead of others, but the practice is devastating to the hillsides and often leads to washed-out trails. A reminder of the damage caused by this, along with a few examples of damage pointed out on the trail, is usually sufficient.

Family Pets

Don't bring them, even if the rules of the trail say you can. Although Rover may like outings as much as other members of the family do, most trails just aren't appropriate for pets, especially if you want to enjoy the plants and animals along the way.

Sharing discoveries is always fun.

Fires

No fires should ever be built in any of the parks mentioned here except in designated sites at campgrounds and picnic areas. This is extremely important, because most of the trails in this guide are in and near habitats that become extremely volatile during the hot, dry months between May and October. Many parks even have rules against smoking on their trails during dry, summer months.

Trail Right-of-Way

While hikers have as much right to the use of the trails in this guide as any other group, simple courtesy and a sense of safety say that hikers should give the right-of-way to mountain bikers and horseback riders. When you hear them coming, step off the trail, wait for them to pass, and avoid any loud noises or sudden movement as they do.

Leave Nothing But Footprints; Take Nothing But Photos

The hikes in this guide are in regional, state, or national parks, all of which have rules about collecting or destroying plants, animals, and other natural items. Help your children understand these rules and why they exist. If you are unsure of what the rules are for any park where you plan to hike, contact the local ranger for information, which they are always glad to furnish.

This is an opportunity to develop a wilderness ethic for your family by emphasizing how parks have been set aside for all to enjoy, and that destruction of plants and animals (and collecting often has the same results as heedless destruction), as well as unsightly littering, defeats that purpose.

ENJOYING NATURE

While hiking can be an end unto itself, most children like to investigate the ins and outs of the world around them, and that includes sites along trails. A creek becomes something more than just a body of water to be crossed. It becomes a place to investigate; a place where smooth, round rocks can be skipped across large pools; insect larvae can be discovered under slimy bottom rocks; frogs can be found in creekside vegetation; and feet can be soaked as energy food is consumed.

The same is true of trees, boulders, and hillsides. All provide many attractions to your children, and you can utilize this interest to introduce the study of nature, and you can do so in a sharing way.

Sharing, Not Teaching

Let your children share in your interests as you walk along the trail and at rest stops. Point out a wildflower that you like. If your child is interested, discuss where the flower grows, what insects are around it, and other particulars that you can observe, and you can do all of these without ever knowing the flower's name.

You don't have to teach the children anything. They can experience it right along with you. And you can experience anew the delight of investigating a creekbed, tree, or bluff through their eyes.

Use All of Your Senses

Watch the light fall across a meadow, smell a pine tree, and touch a thistle. Even taste a limestone rock. All these will give you and your children a variety of sensations with which to experience nature.

Getting the Feel of Nature

When your child complains about the trail being hot and dusty, ask how the various animals in the area cope with the midday heat, and where they get their refreshments. Suggest that the shade of the forest ahead may bring about a change in mood, and offer a drink or a snack to help refresh the spirit as well as the body. Once you get to that shady forest, discuss how the animals that live nearby might enjoy similar breaks during their day.

Relating moods and experiences to the wildlife that lives in the region will help you and your children become more in touch with the natural world, and add immeasurably to your hiking experiences.

With these suggestions, and thoughts of your own, you should be able to find trails in this guide that will give you many hours of pleasant outdoor activity. Go, and enjoy, but first make some pre-hike preparations.

GETTING READY FOR DAYHIKES

While it is possible to simply get in your car and drive to a hiking trail with no preparation, it is not necessarily wise. A little preparation will make all hikes more enjoyable, and may prevent unnecessary trouble.

The Ten Essentials

The Mountaineers recommends ten items that should be taken on every hike, whether a day trip or an overnight. When children are involved, and you are particularly intent on making the trip as trouble-free as possible, these "Ten Essentials" may avert disaster.

1. **Extra clothing.** It may rain, the temperature may drop, or wading may be too tempting to pass up. Be sure to include rain gear, extra shoes and socks (especially a pair of shoes that can be used for wading), a warm sweater, and hat and light gloves.

2. **Extra food.** Extra high-energy snacks are essential for active children and adults. Carry sufficient water in canteens and fanny packs in case no suitable source is available on the trail.

3. **Sunglasses.** Look for a pair that screens UV rays.

4. **Knife.** Chances are you will never need it, but bring one along anyway. A knife with multiple blades, scissors, a bottle opener, and tweezers is a must.

5. **Firestarter—candle or chemical fuel.** If you must build a fire, these are indispensable.

6. **First-aid kit.** Don't forget to include moleskin for blisters, baking soda to apply to stings, and any special medication your child might need if he or she is allergic to bee stings or other insect bites, and extra sunscreen.

7. **Matches in a waterproof container.** You can buy these matches in a store that carries hiking and camping gear.

8. **Flashlight.** Check the batteries before you begin your hike.

9. **Map.** Don't assume you'll just "feel" your way to the summit. Maps are important, and I discuss them more later in this introduction.

10. **Compass.** Teach your children how to use it, too.

In addition to these Ten Essentials the following suggestions will help make hikes more enjoyable.

What to Wear

There is little need for special clothes or shoes for dayhiking in the San Francisco Bay Area. Trails are generally well marked and stable. They don't demand heavy-duty hiking boots, and specialty clothing is rarely called for since we have such an equable climate.

Active wear shoes such as those your children wear to school and play in around home are perfectly adequate. Sneakers, especially high tops, give all the support needed, and have the advantage of being broken in. This helps keep blisters to a minimum, thereby avoiding one of the most uncomfortable aspects of hiking.

To enjoy hiking in the North Bay it is important to wear enough of the right kinds of clothing to keep you comfortable in changing weather. This means layers that can be removed and put back on as the day's weather changes from windy and foggy to sunny and warm—and back again. Because hiking is a year-round activity in the Bay Area, and there are so many micro-climates throughout the North Bay, it is difficult to say exactly what clothing you should carry on any one hike. The only thing certain is that you are likely to need layers of clothes any time of year, on any hike.

Rain gear is generally important only in the winter, with an occasional fall or spring storm, but a hat or cap is useful year-round to protect adults and youth alike from the effects of the sun.

Packs

Not everyone has to have a pack on a dayhike, but children love to carry their own to hold their special items. Adult day packs should be large enough to carry bulky clothing and extra food and drinks, but youngsters can use either day or fanny packs. The only requirement is that the packs should be large enough for some food, small items such as magnifying glasses, individual drinking containers, and layers of clothing that have been removed.

Other Items

Other items you may want to bring along to help make hikes fun include lightweight binoculars (one pair per family should do, but some families have several) for looking at birds and animals, as well as for scouting the trail ahead; a magnifying glass and insect boxes for short-term viewing of small animals and plants; a lightweight camera for recording the trip; and possibly some nature guides to help identify objects in the field as they are observed. You can use your knife to help dig around in old stumps or under rocks when searching for creepy crawlers.

None of these items is essential for the enjoyment of hikes, but all help you and your family explore the world of nature close up, and provide activities that can be pursued during rest breaks and eating times.

Maps

Since these trails are in developed parks, you are unlikely to get lost on any of these hikes, although some of the longer ones do take you away from the most heavily traveled areas of the larger parks. A little common sense, a copy of the park brochure, and an awareness of where the trail is, however, should keep you on track.

Topographic maps with contour lines and marked trails aren't strictly necessary, but can be fun and interesting for children. When combined with an inexpensive compass they can be used to determine your exact position on the trail, as well as provide a new and interesting learning experience.

Topographic maps of the region and compasses, as well as instruction books on how to use them, are sold in most hiking and camping stores in the Bay Area.

Food and Drinks

Outings are a good time to let your children have high-energy foods such as candy bars and other sweet snacks as treats. These can be used as motivation to get to that shady tree up the trail where you can stop for a rest, or over the hump to the top of a ridge. You can also take along other foods such as fruit and high-protein foods that the children like for lunch breaks.

Children like to carry some food in their own packs, but you can hold back special treats until they are needed for motivation.

Remember also that one of the "Ten Essentials" is extra food. Whatever you take on the hike, don't skimp. It is always better to carry extra food home than to have hikers become cranky and disagreeable from hunger.

Another item that you absolutely must not skimp on is fluids. Many of the hikes in this guide can be hot and dry during the summer months, and few have drinking water available.

While sugary and sports drinks are fine for replacing lost fluids, never depend solely on them. On Kevin's sixth birthday we took a group of boys on a hike to Lake Ilsanjo in Annadel State Park, and took along only snack drinks to have with lunch and along the trail. The June day was hot, there was no potable water at the lake, and several of the group complained loudly about their need for "real" water during the five-mile round trip to the lake and back.

First Aid and Safety

First aid and safety are generally big items in hiking books, but in reality I have found that my children have less need for first aid on the trail than during a normal day.

Nevertheless, my "Ten Essentials" first-aid kit includes large and small bandages, antibacterial cream, a squeeze bottle of hydrogen peroxide, a patch of moleskin, some scissors, an athletic bandage, a medicine for relief of insect stings, and some itch medicine. Recently I have also begun carrying a cold wrap, but I must admit this is more for me than for my children.

Though not technically first aid, sunscreen and insect repellant should also be carried. While biting insects aren't a major problem in the Bay Area, there are times when mosquitoes and flies can be bothersome, and the repellent helps. Sunscreen is an absolute necessity, especially for those of us so fair-skinned as to "burn while on the backside of the moon," because many of the trails cover long distances where there is little or no shade.

In addition to the normal scrapes and falls that accompany active children, nature also offers several, if not dangers, at least worries that parents must be aware of, and caution children about.

Poison Oak, Nettles, and Thistles

These are all plants that can precipitate either an immediate or delayed reaction that causes discomfort, and you should be aware of what these plants look like during various seasons.

Stinging nettles cause a more immediate reaction than poison oak (which generally doesn't appear for two days to two weeks after exposure) and can be quite painful—even excruciatingly so—to children and adults alike. Various types of thistles also cause intense pain and itching to some people.

Itch medicines help with, but don't completely relieve, the discomfort of stinging nettles. The best solution is to avoid contact. If you don't know what the various plants look like, park rangers will be glad to help you identify them, and many parks have signs illustrating poison oak and nettles. If you are hiking in areas, such as Point Reyes, where nettles and thistles are abundant, you may want to take along a field guide with which to make a positive identification.

Stinging Insects

Some parks in this guide have large numbers of stinging insects such as yellow jackets, and these can be scary to children. While their stings are painful, they don't have to be cause for ending a hike. Over-the-counter medicines are available that relieve the discomfort when rubbed on a sting.

Rattlesnakes

Rattlesnakes are another fear of parents, and many parks in this guide have large populations of rattlers that come out during the warm spring and hot summer months. Very few hikers ever see these reclusive animals, though, and a few simple precautions are all that are necessary to avoid a bite: Never stick your hand down into rocky crevices without first looking. Never climb rock faces where you have to put your hands into holes for handholds. Always watch where you are stepping when you step over logs and rocks.

Rattlesnakes are poisonous, and they do occasionally bite people, but their bites are seldom fatal. If, by chance, a member of your hiking party is bitten by a rattlesnake, don't panic. Have the person who was bitten lie down, remain still, and send another member of the group to find a ranger or phone. Let the authorities, whether a ranger or 911 operator, know where the victim is located and when the bite occurred. With modern medicine there is little danger if medical attention is given promptly.

Lost and Injured Children

I have tried to emphasize the reality of danger on trails in the Bay Area, but most are minimal. Two dangers, however, stand out above all others, and adults can do much to control them. The first is injury and death from falls around cliffs. Children love to climb on rocks and cliffs and have great fun doing so, but the crumbly sandstone cliffs that are so common along the Bay Area shoreline are the most dangerous that can be found. No one, child or adult, should climb on them because they present definite and immediate danger. Even walking too close to the edge of these cliffs places hikers in danger.

The second danger is of children who stray from the group and become lost and panic-stricken. Search-and-rescue units spend many hours searching for lost children in the chaparral of parks such as Mount Tamalpais, and members often speak to school and youth groups about how to avoid this lonely and terrifying experience. First, they advise that everyone carry a loud whistle. Second, they recommend that anyone separated from the group and unable to gain attention with a whistle, "hug" a tree (or a bush or boulder). This means the child should sit down next to a tree, or bush, or boulder, and stay there until found. The only other action the lost person should take is to blow a whistle or shout loudly at regular intervals.

With these simple precautions and preparations, you should find that hiking the trails of the North Bay counties will be a satisfying way to spend family outings.

NATURAL HISTORY OF THE NORTH BAY

The North Bay includes a wide variety of plant and animal communities, including some, such as the coast redwood forests, that are found only in Northern California. Many hikers enjoy their outings without ever learning anything of significance about the plants or animals that they may encounter on the trail, but I find that I enjoy my outings a little more when I learn something about the various natural communities and how the plants and animals interact with each other. For those who want to learn more about the various plant and animal communities of the North Bay, both the University of California Press and Wilderness Press publish a number of natural history guidebooks that are very useful. The following are a few examples of the flora and fauna that you are likely to see in your wanderings.

Chaparral

Many hills of California are covered by a dense growth of hard-leafed, drought-resistant plants collectively known as *chaparral*. The plants in this community are well adapted to the long dry summers and wet winters

Each plant has its own characteristics.

of Northern California because they tolerate the hot dry spells and protect the hillsides during the wet winter months. In addition, they regenerate very quickly from fires.

The plants in these communities include various species of manzanita, which have shiny red bark on the trunk and branches and range from low creepers to 15-foot-tall shrubs; ceanothus, sometimes called California lilac, with its large clusters of blue or white flowers; and chamise, a member of the rose family that spreads into almost impenetrable thickets that are 2 to 10 feet high.

Coastal Scrub

The plants in these communities are softer than those in chaparral, and the dominant plant is coyote brush. Coastal scrub is found near the ocean and bay where there is more moisture and less heat.

Wildflowers

Wildflowers such as California poppy and blue lupine are familiar to everyone who has driven along the highways of Northern California, but there are dozens more native wildflowers that can be identified along the trails given in this guide.

Trees

Several species of trees are so common in the region that you will probably encounter at least one species on almost every hike in this book. These include the many species of oak that are native to the region (and it is hard for some people to distinguish between these); various species of exotic eucalyptus (which were brought here from Australia in the nineteenth century); bay, which is also known as California laurel, pepperwood, and myrtle; buckeye, a member of the horse-chestnut family; madrone, with its distinctive smooth red trunks and peeling bark; Douglas fir, an important lumber tree that grows to a height of 300 feet; and the coast redwood, the tallest tree in the world.

Mammals

Raccoon, opossum, gray squirrels, chipmunks, ground squirrels, rabbits, coyote, gray fox, bobcat, and black-tailed deer are some of the more common animals that you are either likely to encounter or observe signs of along the trails of North Bay parks. In some parks you may even see signs of bear and cougar, but you're not likely to run into either.

In the parks of Sonoma County you are also likely to run into feral pigs that roam the oak woodlands eating acorns and roots.

None of these presents any danger to hikers, with the possible exception of bear and cougar (and there have been no reports of attacks by either in the Bay Area in many years), and children are delighted to see animals in their natural habitat.

Sea lions and harbor seals are often spotted in and around the bay.

Birds

Various hawks, vultures, jays, and a number of types of gulls are all common in the region, and a bird guide will help you identify the many smaller birds that you will come across on your hikes.

HOW TO USE THIS GUIDE

The hikes in this guide are located in the North Bay counties of Marin, Napa, and Sonoma, and are located within county, state, and federal parks and reserves. Most parks provide maps or brochures that describe the trails within their boundaries and tell something about the natural history of the region. You can obtain these either at the parks or from park district offices. The addresses and phone numbers of park districts are listed at the end of this introduction.

Although the trails in the guide are permanent, there is always the possibility that one will be closed because of a landslide, fire danger, or other natural condition. In addition, park officials sometimes reroute trails or close them temporarily for other reasons.

You can call the park where you intend to hike to ask about the latest trail conditions and find out if the trail you intend to use is open. If it isn't, you can ask about similar trails nearby and most park officials will gladly help.

While the number of hikes in this guide may seem like a lot for the region, they represent less than one-tenth of the total miles of trails that are available in the three counties. Mount Tamalpais State Park alone has more than 250 miles of trails; it is only one of several large parks in the region.

The hikes that are included were selected with several thoughts in mind. One was that there be some hikes that anyone, even those barely past the toddler stage and those who are quite elderly, could enjoy. Another was that the majority be moderate hikes from which most families would derive a sense of accomplishment after completing, and the last was that some be difficult enough to challenge older children (up to 12 years old) in good physical condition who like to hike.

The hikes also cover the wide range of natural habitats that exist in the North Bay. Open grasslands, oak woodlands, mixed oak and madrone forests, mixed conifer forests, redwood and fir forests, tidelands, and seashore are all represented, and you are will see a wide variety of flora and fauna as you walk along the trails.

Entries for the hikes include information about length, difficulty, and location, and tell something about the natural history of the region covered by the trails.

One last thought. This is a guide to dayhikes in the North Bay, but the California Department of Parks and Recreation and the National Park Service have developed a number of environmental campsites at

Angel Island, Mount Tamalpais, Point Reyes, Sonoma Coast State Beaches, and other sites in the region where you can backpack in for one or more nights. These are not covered here, but you may want to investigate the possibilities after you have explored many of the trails and are ready for a more adventurous family outing.

PARK DISTRICT HEADQUARTERS

The following is a listing of the district headquarters of the local, county, regional, state, and national parks where the hikes in this guide are located. If you have any questions about the conditions of the trails—whether it is too wet or hot and dry to hike in the park, what wildflowers are blooming, etc.—give them a call. They are always willing to answer questions or will refer you to someone who can.

Angel Island State Park
P.O. Box 318
Tiburon, CA 94920
415-435-1915

Annadel State Park
6201 Channel Drive
Santa Rosa, CA 95405
707-539-3911

Armstrong Redwoods State Reserve
17000 Armstrong Woods Road
Guerneville, CA 95446
707-869-2015

Bothe–Napa Valley State Park
3801 St. Helena Highway North
Calistoga, CA 94515
707-942-4575

China Camp State Park
P.O. Box 244, Route 1
San Rafael, CA 94901
415-456-0766

Golden Gate National
Recreation Area
Visitor Center, Building 1050
Marin Headlands
Sausalito, CA 94965
415-331-1540

Jack London State Historic Park
P.O. Box 358
Glen Ellen, CA 95442
707-938-5216

Marin County Department
of Parks and Recreation
Civic Center Drive
San Rafael, CA 94901
415-499-6387

Marin Municipal Water District
220 Nellen Avenue
Corte Madera, CA 94925
415-924-4600

Mount Tamalpais State Park
801 Panoramic Highway
Mill Valley, CA 94941
415-388-2070

Muir Woods National Monument
Mill Valley, CA 94941
415-388-2595

Olompali State Historic Park
P.O. Box 244, Route 1
San Rafael, CA 94901
415-456-0766

Point Reyes National Seashore
Point Reyes, CA 94956
415-663-1092

Samuel P. Taylor State Park
P.O. Box 251
Lagunitas, CA 94938
415-488-9897

Sonoma Coast State Beach
Bodega Bay, CA 94923
707-875-3483

Sonoma County Department
of Parks and Recreation
2403 Professional Drive, Ste. 100
Santa Rosa, CA 95403
707-527-2041

Sugarloaf Ridge State Park
2605 Adobe Canyon Road
Kenwood, CA 95452
707-833-5712

Tomales Bay State Park
Star Route
Inverness, CA 94937
415-669-1140

A NOTE ABOUT SAFETY

Safety is an important concern in all outdoor activities. No guidebook can alert you to every hazard or anticipate the limitations of every reader. Therefore, the descriptions of roads, trails, routes, and natural features in this book are not representations that a particular place or excursion will be safe for your party. When you follow any of the routes described in this book, you assume responsibility for your own safety. Under normal conditions, such excursions require the usual attention to traffic, road and trail conditions, weather, terrain, the capabilities of your party, and other factors. Keeping informed on current conditions and exercising common sense are the keys to a safe, enjoyable outing.

The Mountaineers

Acknowledgments

Although I did all the writing for this guide, my nine-year-old son Kevin is listed as coauthor, and for a very good reason. Without his interest in hiking and nature it may very well have never been written. As a companion on the trail, and as a constant push at home (especially when he attempted to compute what his share of the income from the book would be), Kevin has played an important role from start to finish.

My wife Mary also deserves mention, for she has been a trail companion for more than twenty years, even though she prefers what she describes as "Midwest walks" where there are few hills, which sometimes conflicts with my desire to reach the highest spot around. Her suggestions on what to include in the trail entries were taken seriously, except that her idea to include information about trails where you can take dogs was discarded, because pets should not be brought along when hiking.

Finally I wish to thank the people at The Mountaineers for giving me the opportunity to share some of my favorite hikes with others.

LEGEND

═══	MAJOR ROAD
▬▬▬	SECONDARY ROAD, PAVED
══	UNPAVED ROAD
====	FIRE ROAD, JEEP TRAIL (NO MOTOR VEHICLES)
••••••	HIKING ROUTE
•—•—•	PAVED TRAIL
----	OTHER TRAIL
Ⓣ⒯	TRAILHEAD
Ⓟ	PARKING
→	DIRECTION OF HIKE
▲	CAMPGROUND
⊼	PICNIC SITE
o═o	GATE
)(	FOOTBRIDGE
~···~	RIVER OR STREAM
⸜⸝	MARSH
⋇	SUMMIT OR PEAK
⊦⊦⊦⊦⊦⊦⊦⊦	RAILROAD RIGHT OF WAY
⊢—⊣	BENCH

Key to Symbols

 Dayhikes. These are hikes that can be completed in a single day. While some trips allow camping, only a few require it.

 Easy trails. These are relatively short, smooth, gentle trails suitable for small children or first-time hikers.

 Moderate trails. Most of these are 2 to 4 miles total distance and feature more than 500 feet of elevation gain. The trail may be rough and uneven. Hikers should wear lug-soled boots and be sure to carry the Ten Essentials.

 Difficult trails. These are often rough, with considerable elevation gain or distance to travel. They are suitable for older or experienced children. Lug-soled boots and the Ten Essentials are standard equipment.

 Hikable. The best times of year to hike each trail are indicated by the following symbols: flower—spring; sun—summer; leaf—fall; snowflake—winter.

 Driving directions. These paragraphs tell you how to get to the trailheads.

 Turnarounds. These are places, mostly along moderate trails, where families can cut their hike short yet still have a satisfying outing. Turnarounds usually offer picnic opportunities, views, or special natural attractions.

 Cautions. These mark potential hazards—cliffs, stream or highway crossing, and the like—where close supervision of children is strongly recommended.

 Environmental close-ups. These highlight special environmental elements along the trail and help children learn about and respect nature.

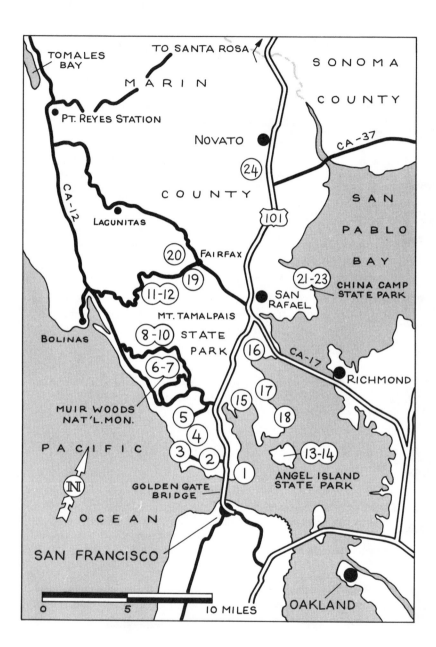

TO SANTA ROSA

TOMALES BAY

MARIN

SONOMA

COUNTY

PT. REYES STATION

NOVATO

CA-37

24

101

SAN

PABLO

BAY

CA-12

LAGUNITAS

COUNTY

20

FAIRFAX

19

21-23

CHINA CAMP
STATE PARK

11-12

SAN
RAFAEL

MT. TAMALPAIS

BOLINAS

8-10

STATE

PARK

16

CA-17

6-7

15

17

RICHMOND

MUIR WOODS
NAT'L. MON.

5

18

PACIFIC

4

3

2

13-14

N

1

ANGEL ISLAND
STATE PARK

GOLDEN GATE
BRIDGE

OCEAN

SAN FRANCISCO

0   5   10 MILES

OAKLAND

Southern Marin

Everyone needs a rest stop occasionally.

Vistas of the open ocean and the Golden Gate lead hikers out to Lime Point.

1. Bay Trail to Lime Point

Type:	Dayhike
Difficulty:	Easy for children
Distance:	1 mile, round trip
Hiking time:	1 hour
Elevation gain:	Level
Hikable:	Year-round
Map:	Rambler's Guide to Trails of Mt. Tamalpais and the Marin Headlands, Olmsted & Brothers Map Company

This trail is closed temporarily for an environmental cleanup. Contact Golden Gate National Recreation Area (415-331-1540) for information about reopening.

This short hike at the beginning of the Bay Trail in the Golden Gate National Recreation Area (GGNRA) takes you underneath the north tower of the Golden Gate Bridge and gives spectacular views of San Francisco Bay and the Golden Gate. Several close offshore rocks are roosting sites for a variety of seabirds, and the trail passes by rock outcroppings that are examples of geological uplifting and folding.

Take the Alexander Avenue exit off US 101 north of the bridge, bear left at the GGNRA sign, and swing right on Bunker Road just before the tunnel to Fort Cronkhite. Continue on Bunker Road to Fort Baker, go past the fishing pier toward the bridge tower. Park in the lot just to the east of the bridge where there are picnic tables.

This short hike over an easy trail is often warm and clear when areas to the west of the bridge are fog shrouded. But the winds do pick up as you reach the end of the trail on the seaward side of the bridge at Lime Point, which looks out toward the open ocean.

Seabirds often sit on nearby rocks that jut up from the bay; harbor seals sometimes come near shore; wildflowers dot the hillside during spring, and outcroppings show the violent geological history of the region. Folds and uplifts are very evident in outcroppings on the west side of the trail at about 0.25 mile from the beginning and also directly beneath the bridge at the base of the north tower.

Have your children guess how the folds and uplifts along the trail came about. Then demonstrate how the folds and uplifts occurred by taking a leaf or piece of paper and pushing toward the middle from each end. The way the leaf or paper bends, folds, and cracks is very similar to what occurred when the San Andreas Fault pushed against the layers of sedimentary rocks that are now exposed beside the trail.

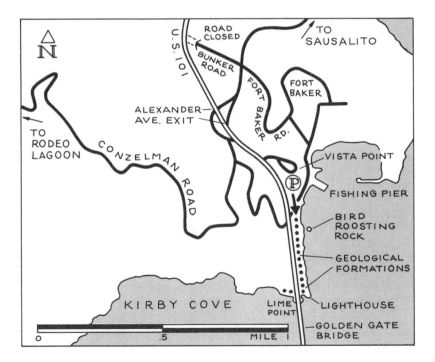

2. Coast Trail to Slacker Hill

Type:	Dayhike
Difficulty:	Moderate to difficult for children
Distance:	4 miles, round trip
Hiking time:	2 to 3 hours
Elevation gain:	600 feet
Hikable:	Year-round
Map:	Rambler's Guide to Trails of Mt. Tamalpais and the Marin Headlands, Olmsted & Brothers Map Company

This section of the Coast Trail, which is also an integral link in the proposed 400-mile-long Bay Ridge Trail, offers panoramic views of San Francisco Bay, Alcatraz, the San Francisco skyline, Rodeo Lagoon, and the open ocean. On a clear day, the Farallon Islands are visible from the top of Slacker Hill. The trail leads up the east side of the ridge and passes through open grassland and low scrub. Thirty-five different wildflowers have been identified along the trail, and birds are plentiful during breeding times. A special feature of the trail is that it leads through a narrow funnel in the West Coast migration route of raptors. Raptors are large birds that seize their prey by diving down from the sky. They include hawks, owls, and eagles.

The trail begins from a large parking lot on the west side of US 101 at the north end of the Golden Gate Bridge. This lot is across the freeway from the more popular Vista Point parking lot and can be reached by taking the Alexander Avenue exit when heading north. Double back under the freeway at the first left turn and go up Conzelman Road. A short way uphill, turn left into the parking lot. If you're going south on US 101, take the Conzelman Road exit and turn left into the lot.

Broad wooden steps at the trail head lead from the parking lot into a cypress grove. As you leave the trees, the trail takes a wide turn uphill, and at 0.25 mile crosses Conzelman Road. Crosswalk lines indicate the direction of the trail. As you climb, the sounds of automobiles on the bridge and freeway slowly diminish, and you enter into a world of raptors, grassland, and Monarch butterflies, who stop over on the low bushes on the hillsides during their fall migration south.

The panorama from the trail includes all of the bay to the east and the rainbow entrance to Waldo Tunnel to the north. Outcroppings of sedimentary rocks show signs of folding and uplifting near the tunnel.

The Coastal Trail leads through a grove of cypress before reaching open country.

At about 0.75 mile you come to a spring that seeps out of the hillside above the trail and a short bridge that leads over a small creek. The water attracts a variety of birds and animals, and the surrounding growth supports many nesting birds during breeding season. Deer, bobcat, coyote, and badger signs are frequently evident along this section of the trail.

A little past 1 mile, you come to another seep, a bridge over a larger creek that runs most of the year (all year in wet times), and plenty of bracken ferns, sawgrass, alder, and willow. Again, signs of wildlife are plentiful. Both of these spots are excellent rest stops that offer interesting views.

At both springs search for signs of the animals that come for water. Raccoons leave tracks about 2 inches long that look like small hands. Deer tracks look like half an oval divided in two parts, and bobcat tracks look like large house cat tracks. Scat, or feces, of these animals is also frequently found near the springs. Try to guess what animal left scat if you find it. Does it look like that of a cat? If it does, it might have been from a bobcat. If it looks like that of a dog, it was probably from a coyote.

The trail is mostly uphill to the first spring, but levels out for a short stretch before heading back up after the second spring. It reaches a saddle at about 1.25 miles where it intersects with the SCA Trail. This is a good turnaround point if anyone in the party is tired, but most will

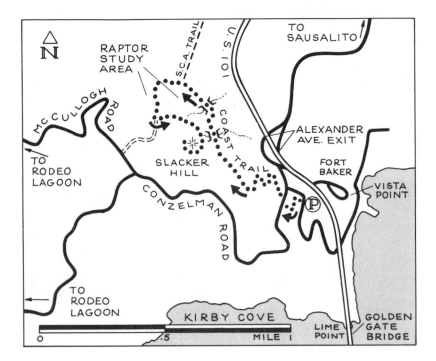

want to turn left toward Rodeo Lagoon. This new trail is wider, and mountain bikers are allowed on it. Watch and listen for them as you go around corners.

At about 1.5 miles you reach the top of the ridge and can see Rodeo Lagoon in the distance, as well as much of the Marin Headlands. At this point you enter a hawk migration study area, and the scientists conducting the study ask that you not linger along or leave the trail in the study area between August 15 and December 15. The trail leads through the highest concentration of migrating raptors in the West, and you will be tempted to stand and observe these birds of prey as they skim the tops of the ridges around you.

About 200 yards downhill from the study area an old road leads uphill to the left. This road circles the study area to the south and ends at the top of Slacker Hill, which is an excellent picnic area, with a large flat area providing a 360-degree view of San Francisco, the bay, and Marin, but it can be cold and windy. Hawks are also easily spotted here, even after the migration season has ended.

You return by the same trails.

---

3. Rodeo Lagoon Trail Loop

Type: Dayhike
Difficulty: Easy for children
Distance: 1.5 miles, loop
Hiking time: 1 hour
Elevation gain: Minimal
Hikable: Year-round
Map: Rambler's Guide to Trails of Mt. Tamalpais and the Marin Headlands, Olmsted & Brothers Map Company

This is an excellent hike for those just beginning nature hikes with young children, or for those who wish a good introduction to the natural history of the Marin Headlands. Rodeo Lagoon in the Golden Gate National Recreational Area is a natural lagoon formed by beach buildup. It generally catches fresh water that flows down the valley from ridges above, but waves occasionally wash over the beach during winter storms, forming brackish water.

Follow the driving directions for hike 2, Coast Trail to Slacker Hill,

Rodeo Lagoon and Beach offer many choices to young hikers.

but continue on Conzelman Road for about 1 mile. Turn right on McCullough Road for less than a mile, and then turn left on Bunker Road and continue for 2 miles to the parking area.

Rodeo Beach is often a surprise for first-time visitors because it is covered with tiny, multicolored pebbles. These are primarily chert and greenstone. The reddish chert is a hard sedimentary rock that does not break down into sand particles, and a barrier of this extends about 1500 feet out into the ocean from the beach and protects the beach from strong wave action.

In addition to chert and greenstone, those interested in rocks can find jasper, carnelian, agate, and other semiprecious stones along the beach. Park rules prohibit collecting, so look only, don't take. Children

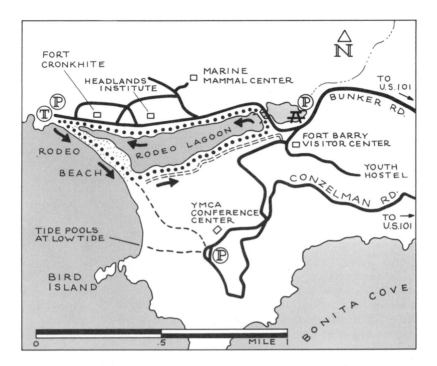

love to play with the many small pebbles on the beach. Have them see how many different colored pebbles they can find, and see if anyone can find one of the rare carnelians, which are a deep orange-red unlike any other pebble found here. (The beach was once named Carnelian Beach.)

The Rodeo Lagoon Trail Loop can be started at the picnic area or the visitor center. It circles the lagoon and also follows a section of the beach. A footbridge crosses a creek at the end of the lagoon away from the ocean, by the picnic area.

Rodeo Lagoon, which is about 0.5 mile long and 0.25 mile wide, is an important stop on the migration routes of many birds, hence, birdwatching is popular here. Canvasback, bufflehead, and merganser ducks can be seen in large numbers during fall and winter. Brown pelicans and cormorants are plentiful during the summer months, when they can be seen in one of their favorite resting spots, Bird Island, off shore from the lagoon.

Guided walks are led from the visitor center, and the displays there help you learn about the natural history of the area. The California Marine Mammal Center, a nonprofit facility licensed to rescue and rehabilitate sick or injured marine mammals, is located behind the visitor center and offers visitors a chance to view some of the animals being rehabilitated, as well as an occasional tour of the facility.

4. Bobcat-Miwok Trail Loop

Type:	Dayhike
Difficulty:	Difficult for children
Distance:	5 miles, loop
Hiking time:	4 hours
Elevation gain:	800 feet
Hikable:	Year-round
Map:	Rambler's Guide to Trails of Mt. Tamalpais and the Marin Headlands, Olmsted & Brothers Map Company

Gerbode Valley, which this trail loop circles, is a nature preserve in the Golden Gate National Recreation Area. Hikers can expect to see evidence of a variety of animals such as rabbits, deer, fox, coyote, and bobcat. The stream that runs down the center of the valley is also an outstanding bird habitat. During spring and early summer, wildflowers bloom profusely alongside the trail.

Follow the directions for Rodeo Lagoon, hike 3. About 1 mile before you come to the visitor center there is an old, unmarked road that curves off Bunker Road to the north. Park at the west end of the old road and look for a trail that leads to two footbridges that cross the creek. This leads to the Rodeo Valley Trail.

Turn left on Rodeo Valley Trail and continue for just under 0.5 mile until Rodeo Valley Trail meets Bobcat Trail. Redwing blackbirds and marsh hawks are frequently seen along this section of the trail, and Bobcat Trail runs uphill from another creek where birds are plentiful for another 0.5 mile. The trail continues uphill at a gentle grade and passes an old ranch house at about 1.5 miles where there are several species of exotic trees, including a stand of eucalyptus. Take a little side trip to the eucalyptus trees to have the children crush some of the leaves and notice the distinctive smell given off by the oil in the leaves. Also look for seed pods of the eucalyptus, which look almost like fancy buttons.

After you pass the ranch house, you'll see hillsides covered with lupine, poppies, paintbrush, morning glory, and many other native flowers during the spring and early summer. Have the children keep track of how many different colored flowers they can spot if there are a lot of blooms. Along this stretch of trail you can look back over Rodeo Lagoon,

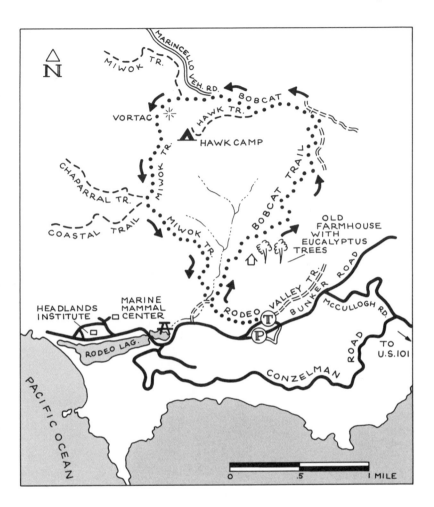

Fort Barry, and the ocean. To the north you can see a grove of pines where Hawk Camp, an environmental campsite, is located.

At about 2 miles you reach the crest of the ridge, a good turnaround site if you or the kids are getting tired, and Bobcat Trail is joined by the Rodeo Valley Trail from the right. Bobcat Trail curves west at this junction, and the three peaks of Mount Tamalpais come into view. Soon you can see Strawberry Point, Richardson Bay, and Tiburon to the north, and the top of the Golden Gate Bridge towers to the south.

As you pass the trail to Hawk Camp you can see the VORTAC, a large white dome that is a homing device for commercial aircraft. Before you reach the summit where the VORTAC sits, you'll pass a sign for the

Rolling hills and open grasslands of the Marin Headlands offer pleasant hikes during the hot summer months.

 Miwok Trail to the north—do not take this because it leads to Tennessee Valley. Continue clockwise around the VORTAC fence to connect with the portion of the Miwok Trail heading south back to Rodeo Lagoon.

The trail is downhill from here until it connects with Bobcat Trail. At this junction, turn left and head back up Bobcat for a short distance until you come to the junction with Rodeo Valley Trail. Return to the bridges that lead to the old road and your car.

5. Tennessee Valley

Type:	Dayhike
Difficulty:	Moderate for children
Distance:	4 miles, round trip
Hiking time:	2 hours
Elevation gain:	200 feet
Hikable:	Year-round
Map:	Rambler's Guide to Trails of Mt. Tamalpais and the Marin Headlands, Olmsted & Brothers Map Company

This popular trail in the Golden Gate National Recreation Area follows a small creek down a valley between 1029-foot Wolf Ridge to the south and 1031-foot Coyote Ridge to the north to Tennessee Cove, where a narrow beach is surrounded by rugged cliffs.

Take the Stinson Beach exit from US 101 to Shoreline Highway. About 0.5 mile from US 101, turn left onto Tennessee Valley Road and follow it to the end, where parking is available.

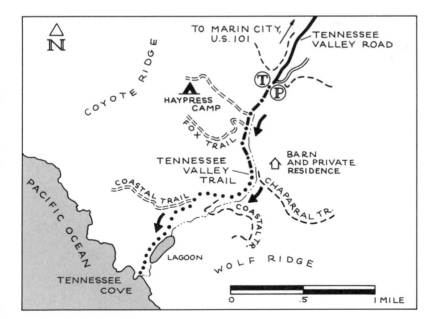

The Tennessee Valley hike begins on a broad paved trail.

This is one of the most popular walks in the Marin Headlands, and it is easy to see why. The trail is smooth, nearly level, and easy for all. It begins as a paved road, soon turns into a gravel road, and finally becomes a footpath.

In the 1960s a plan existed to build a community with 400 acres of high-rise apartments, 500 acres of commercial development, and 175 acres of light industry on the open meadows and hillsides of the Marin Headlands in this area. Until 1978 red-tiled pseudo-mission-style gates stood at the beginning of the trail as testimony to what would have been called Marincello. Local conservationists fought strenuously in a successful effort to keep the hills and valleys undeveloped. The developers dropped their proposal and the area was purchased for park land. Have the children try to picture what the area would look like if all of the proposed development had been completed.

The Miwok Trail runs north and south across the trailhead of the Tennessee Valley Trail, and several other trails, including the Coastal Trail, cross it before you reach the ocean. These cross trails offer hikers further opportunity to explore the hills of the Marin Headlands. The trail follows along the banks of a creek where children can search for small water animals.

Just before you reach Tennessee Cove you pass by an artificial lagoon, which is generally full of ducks and home to many small birds. Children like to see how many different kinds of water birds they can spot here. Have them compare the eating habits of the water birds and the many small birds that live in the low-lying plants that grow along the edges of the lagoon.

The small beach at the cove is surrounded by large cliffs. Notice how the many shorebirds that can be seen near the beach differ from the water birds at the lagoon. Have the children compare how the two types of birds are alike and how they are different.

This is an excellent site for a picnic or rest before you return the way you came to the parking area.

6. Redwoods Grove Trail Loop

Type:	Dayhike
Difficulty:	Easy for children
Distance:	2 miles, loop
Hiking time:	1 hour
Elevation gain:	Level
Hikable:	Year-round
Map:	Rambler's Guide to Trails of Mt. Tamalpais and the Marin Headlands, Olmsted & Brothers Map Company

Muir Woods National Monument is one of the most popular tourist attractions in Marin County and has some of the most stringent restrictions of any park in this guide: You may not ride motor vehicles, horses, or bicycles; bring pets of any kind; or even picnic within the boundaries of the monument. Is it worth a dayhike? Most assuredly, for its 580 acres contain the world's most famous redwood grove, and even on a crowded summer weekend you can find solitude away from the masses. Midweek hikes are much more enjoyable, though, for that is when the majestic redwoods, which reach up to 253 feet in the grove; the creek, which has rushing rapids complete with spawning salmon in winter and quiet pools in the summer; and the canyon, with its fern-covered sides, provide a wonderful buffer from the bustling world just across the ridge.

Take CA-1 off US 101 at the Stinson Beach exit. Continue west for 3 very winding miles to Panoramic Highway; go right for 1 mile to Muir Woods Road. Turn left and continue 1.5 miles to the parking lot, which will resemble a shopping center parking lot on sunny weekends.

Muir Woods National Monument has plenty of scenic spots.

The trail from the parking lot to the visitor center passes markers pointing out the more common plants found in the redwood forests, and on the west side of Redwood Creek across from the center, accessible by a wooden bridge, is a 0.25-mile-long nature trail in Bohemian Grove. At the end of the nature trail another footbridge crosses to the east side of the creek where you enter Cathedral Grove.

Another 0.25 mile takes you to the William Kent Memorial Tree, a 273-foot Douglas fir, which is the tallest tree in the monument. This tree is enormous by any standard, and children like to try to see how many people it takes to put their arms around it. You may also have them guess how many people it would take, standing on each other's shoulders, to be as tall as the tree. You can backtrack along the east side of the creek and continue south to the visitor center, passing a memorial to Gifford Pinchot, an early conservationist.

This hike is completely within the monument so you cannot enjoy a picnic, but you can stop for a snack and a cup of coffee at the visitor center.

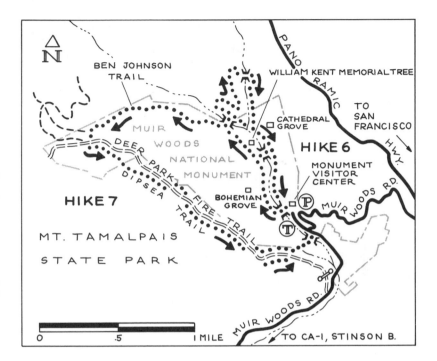

7. Ben Johnson Trail Loop

Type:	Dayhike
Difficulty:	Difficult for children
Distance:	4.5 miles, loop
Hiking time:	3 hours
Elevation gain:	900 feet
Hikable:	Year-round
Map:	Rambler's Guide to Trails of Mt. Tamalpais and the Marin Headlands, Olmsted & Brothers Map Company

While the Redwood Groves Trail Loop introduces hikers to many sites in the monument, it does not necessarily take you away from the crowds of tourists that can be found on nice days. The Ben Johnson Trail

The Ben Johnson Trail leads up and away from the crowds of the monument floor.

Loop, also in Muir Woods National Monument, does. In addition to the redwoods, this loop offers spectacular views, no crowds, and an opportunity to stop along the way for a picnic.

 Directions to Muir Woods National Monument can be found in hike 6, the Redwood Groves Trail Loop.

Begin your hike at the visitor center, enter the nature trail in Bohemian Grove, and go to the intersection of the nature trail and Hillside Trail. Take a left on Hillside Trail, which takes you away from Redwood Creek. The trail rises gently as it moves away from the creek, and at about 0.5 mile it dead ends into Ben Johnson Trail.

From here the trail heads uphill, offering spectacular views to the east. At a little less than 1.5 miles, the Ben Johnson Trail takes a sharp left and soon intersects with the Stapleveldt Trail. Continuing on the Ben Johnson Trail, you will soon cross the Deer Park Fire Trail and dead end on the Dipsea Trail. Turn left on the Dipsea Trail and head back downhill.

After about 0.25 mile along the Dipsea Trail, you will exit the monument and enter Mount Tamalpais State Park. You can picnic along the next 1-mile stretch, but watch for poison oak as you descend the trail. The poison oak can be distinguished from the rest of the brush by its shiny, lobed (meaning that the leaves have small, rounded points) leaves that are attached to the stem in groups of three. The leaves are very similar in shape and appearance to oak leaves, although smaller, and have a reddish tinge as they come out in the spring. They are a bright red in the fall as they get ready to drop.

The Dipsea crosses the Deer Park Fire Trail three times on the descent, and just after the third crossing it splits into two separate trails. (Have the children keep track of how many times you have crossed the fire trail so they have an idea of how much farther they have to go.) Take either trail because they meet in less than 0.25 mile, and shortly you reenter the monument.

About 0.25 mile after reentering the monument, you will cross Redwood Creek and come to a paved road. Turn left on this and continue
0.25 mile back to the parking lot.

8. Verna Dunshee Trail Loop

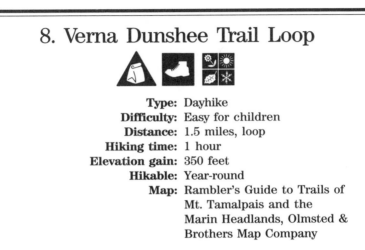

Type:	Dayhike
Difficulty:	Easy for children
Distance:	1.5 miles, loop
Hiking time:	1 hour
Elevation gain:	350 feet
Hikable:	Year-round
Map:	Rambler's Guide to Trails of Mt. Tamalpais and the Marin Headlands, Olmsted & Brothers Map Company

Mount Tamalpais is the dominating physical feature of Marin County,
and on one of the rare clear days, from East Peak you can see the snow-
covered peaks of the Sierra Nevada 200 miles away. Because of its breathtaking panoramas that include Tiburon, Mount Diablo, the Marin Headlands, the San Francisco skyline, and the Farallon Islands 26 miles out
into the Pacific Ocean, Mount Tamalpais has been a popular hiking
destination for San Francisco residents since the 1880s, when they had
to take a ferry to reach the North Bay region.

Today Mount Tamalpais State Park offers more than 200 miles of
trails that cross grass-covered hills, wander along stream banks, venture
into damp redwood canyons where waterfalls flow in torrents over rocks
and boulders, and break through chaparral on sun-baked slopes. The
hikes described here are only a selection of many hikes you can take.

To reach the East Peak visitor center and parking lot take CA-1 off
US 101 at the Stinson Beach exit. Leave CA-1 after 3 winding miles, and
turn right on Panoramic Highway. Follow the signs to Mount Tamalpais
past the Muir Woods Road and Mill Valley intersection, and parking lots
for Mountain Home, Bootjack, and Pantoll to Southside Road. Turn right
on Southside Road and continue 1 mile to Ridgecrest Boulevard. Turn
right on Ridgecrest and go 3 miles to the parking lot.

The Verna Dunshee Trail Loop includes the best vista points on
Mount Tamalpais and is an easy trek for young and old alike. Begin at

the visitor center and follow the paved trail counterclockwise around the peak. At about 0.25 mile you can stop at some benches and view the East Bay and Mount Diablo if the smog is not too thick. Continue on for several hundred yards where you cross a wooden bridge. Look up at the rocks above; you will almost always see some rock climbers scaling the granite boulders.

At just less than 0.5 mile a poorly marked trail leads off to the right to the North Knee of Mount Tamalpais, and you must grapple your way through the hard, sharp chaparral plants that cover the short ridge. Children like this side trip because it takes them away from the easily traveled trail and becomes an adventure.

Although the trail to the North Knee is not well marked, it is easy to follow since the ridge is narrow, and you head down a steep slope if you wander away from the trail. After you reach the Knee, which juts up out of the chaparral, you return to the main trail by the same route.

As you come back to the main trail, you enter an area with larger plants and trees that offer some shade on hot days, making this a good spot to take a break.

Continuing on around the peak you have views of the vast undeveloped forested area owned by the Marin Municipal Water District, and two of the district's five lakes. The largest is Bon Tempe, and nearby is the smaller Lagunitas.

The Verna Dunshee Trail ends near the visitor center, but you can take a sharp left turn onto the 0.2-mile trail to the 2571-foot summit of East Peak where Gardner Lookout sits. Be forewarned before starting up this trail with your little ones that all of the 350-foot elevation gain is on this short section of the trail.

Plenty of picnic sites, restrooms, water, and snacks are available at the visitor center.

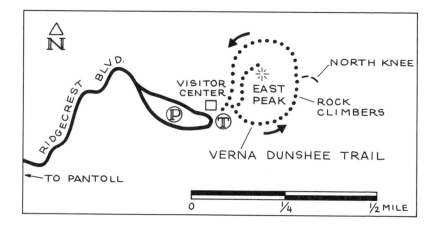

Views from Mount Tamalpais are a photographer's dream.

The trail down Steep Ravine leads to fantastic views of the ocean and shoreline.

9. Steep Ravine Trail to Stinson Beach

Type:	Dayhike
Difficulty:	Moderate to difficult for children
Distance:	3 miles, one way
Hiking time:	3 hours
Elevation loss:	1100 feet
Hikable:	Year-round
Map:	Rambler's Guide to Trails of Mt. Tamalpais and the Marin Headlands, Olmsted & Brothers Map Company

Steep Ravine in Mount Tamalpais State Park is formed by Webb Creek and offers hikers large redwoods, waterfalls, and views of the ocean. During early spring the rushing creek cascades over numerous waterfalls, and wildflowers, particularly trilliums, abound on its banks. Ferns of many kinds (sword, five-finger, spreading wood, woodwardia, and others) cover the creek banks and hang from the trees and rocks.

Follow the directions to East Peak given for hike 8, Verna Dunshee Trail Loop, but stop at the Pantoll Ranger Station and parking lot. A sign indicating the Steep Ravine Trail is at the south end of the parking lot.

The first 0.5 mile of the trail switches back through a forest of redwood, fir, and bay until its reaches Webb Creek and a footbridge. In the next mile you cross several footbridges, descend several steep grades by means of steps, and climb down one ladder as the creek drops precipitously down the ravine. The trail is not dangerous, but it is steep and slippery in spots. You can prepare the children in your group for the steep decline after crossing the first bridge by having them anticipate where the following bridges, steps, and ladder will be by listening for rapids in the creek during times when the water is flowing heavily or by looking for other signs that the trail is beginning to drop more rapidly.

After 1.5 miles, the Steep Ravine trail is joined by the Dipsea Trail, which crosses a footbridge just east of the Steep Ravine Trail.

You have several choices at this point. You can continue on the Steep Ravine Trail for another mile to Rocky Point. To reach this windswept point, continue down the Dipsea Trail about 30 yards past a dam, which is 50 yards from the junction of the two trails. The Steep Ravine Trail

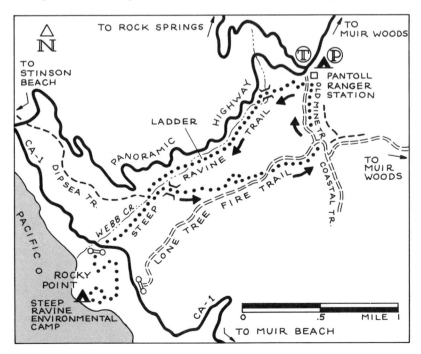

branches off the Dipsea Trail and continues over CA-1 to Rocky Point.

Another choice is to turn back up the Dipsea Trail, continue uphill for about 3 miles to the Old Mine Trail, and on another mile to the parking lot at Pantoll. This is a strenuous climb, however, so be prepared.

The third choice is to keep right on the Dipsea and head on down to the seaside town of Stinson Beach. From there you can take a Golden Gate Transit Bus back to Pantoll.

Those who hike on to Rocky Point can return to the Dipsea Trail and head on into Stinson Beach, or up the Dipsea Trail to the Old Mine Trail, and back to Pantoll.

If you choose to hike to Stinson Beach to catch a bus back to Pantoll, you should contact the Golden Gate Transit Authority at 415-332-6600 for bus schedules from Stinson Beach to Pantoll.

---

10. Benstein/Cataract Trail Loop

Type: Dayhike
Difficulty: Moderate for children
Distance: 3.5 miles, loop
Hiking time: 3 hours
Elevation gain: 300 feet
Hikable: Year-round
Map: Rambler's Guide to Trails of Mt. Tamalpais and the Marin Headlands, Olmsted & Brothers Map Company

This trail loop gives hikers an opportunity to view many of the features to be found on Mount Tamalpais, and nowhere else on the mountain are the outcroppings of serpentine as good. Serpentine is the metamorphosed peridotite that is California's state rock. These rocks were originally part of the deep ocean floor, and outcroppings are found only in highly disrupted zones in coastal ranges and the Sierra Nevada. While serpentine can be almost any color, most of that found on Mount Tamalpais is gray-green. The final leg of the loop that leads up Cataract Creek is one of the most picturesque on the mountain and has an enchanted forest quality.

    To reach the trailhead follow the directions to East Peak given in hike 8, Verna Dunshee Trail Loop, until you reach the Rock Springs parking lot. A sign about 100 yards north of the parking lot indicates the beginning of the Benstein Trail.

Even those who are only young at heart enjoy local trails.

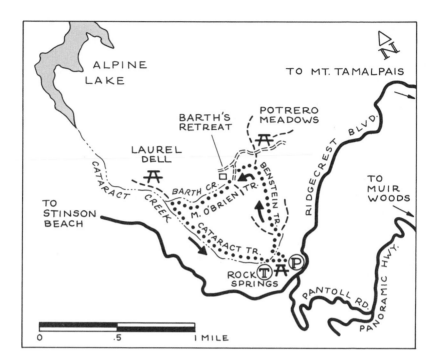

The trail leads down a series of steps and through a forest of Douglas fir, madrone, coast live oak, and canyon live oak for a little over 0.5 mile, where it briefly joins with the Rock Springs–Lagunitas Fire Road. The trail veers off to the left, and leads to the crest of a ridge. About 200 feet past the crest the dense manzanita breaks, and a short trail leads to a vista of the ocean, with views of the Farallon Islands on clear days.

As the trail descends, at about 1 mile it enters a grove of giant chinquapins, trees with yellow underleaves and conspicuous spiny burrs. Soon afterward the vegetation changes, and there is a grove of pygmy Sargent cypress. This is the first indication of a serpentine area where vegetation is limited in both variety and size. Serpentine is deficient in elements such as calcium that most plants need to survive, and contains magnesium, which is toxic to others. Some species, such as the Sargent cypress, grow only on or near serpentine soil.

The trail soon comes to a T just past 1.5 miles in the midst of the chaparral. If you wish to take a break and picnic, turn left and take the trail about 200 yards to Potrero Meadows. Return to the T to continue your hike, and turn right onto the Mickey O'Brien Trail. (If you do not wish to take a break, simply take the trail to the left at the T and continue.) This connecting trail leads through a cool and shady forest, passes Barth's Retreat, and at 2.25 miles dead ends into the Cataract Trail.

You have two choices at this junction. You can turn right on the Cataract Trail and go about 100 yards to the Laurel Dell picnic area (and come back to the junction after your rest stop), or you can turn left to begin the ascent back to Rock Springs.

The trail leads up Cataract Creek past waterfalls and fern-covered hillsides, and around moss-covered boulders. Children can look under the ferns for small flowers, try to find as many different kinds of ferns as they can (there are at least five different ones along this stretch of trail), and watch leaves and small sticks fly over the falls and land below.

There is another picnic area at the Rock Springs parking lot.

---

11. Phoenix Lake Trail Loop

Type: Dayhike
Difficulty: Easy for children
Distance: 1.5 miles, loop
Hiking time: 1.5 hours
Elevation gain: Minimal
Hikable: Year-round
Map: Rambler's Guide to Trails of
Mt. Tamalpais and the
Marin Headlands, Olmsted &
Brothers Map Company

The Marin Municipal Water District has five storage lakes on the north slope of Mount Tamalpais that supply water to Marin residents. These lakes also provide excellent hiking for families. This side of the mountain is generally cooler, shadier, wetter, and wilder than the more populated south side. Although the trails immediately adjacent to the lakes are busy, you can hike for a whole day on some of the outlying trails without encountering another person. Trails connect Phoenix, Lagunitas, and Bon Tempe lakes for longer hikes.

To reach Phoenix Lake take the Sir Francis Drake Boulevard exit off US 101. Follow Sir Francis Drake into Ross, and turn left on Lagunitas Road. Follow Lagunitas to the Natalie Coffin Greene City Park parking lot. The trailhead is a short distance southwest of the parking lot.

Phoenix is a small lake, and the walk around it is easy any season of the year. It offers wildflowers and nesting birds in the spring, active birds and fishing in the summer, colorful leaves in the fall, and cascading creeks in the winter.

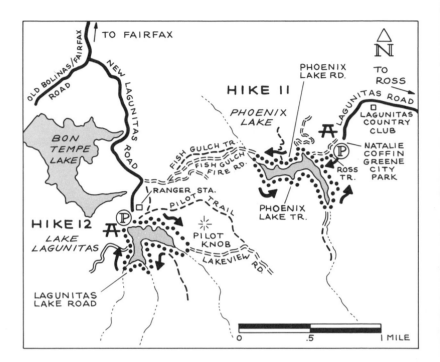

The south side of the lake is an excellent site for ferns. Many varieties can be found there in the winter.

Since the north side and south side of the lake have such different vegetation, you may want to have the children note what types of plants (more grasses and hard brush) grow along the more exposed, dry northern shore, and compare them with those (ferns and soft brush) that grow on the protected, damp southern shore.

For a longer hike take Fish Gulch Trail from the west end of Phoenix Lake to Lagunitas Lake. This 1-mile trail climbs a little over 600 feet and takes about 1 hour. If you take the side trail to Lagunitas Lake, you return to the Phoenix Lake Trail by the same route, and continue on around Phoenix Lake to complete the loop.

There is a picnic area in Natalie Coffin Greene Park.

12. Lake Lagunitas Trail Loop

Type: Dayhike
Difficulty: Easy for children
Distance: 1.5 miles, loop
Hiking time: 1.5 hours
Elevation gain: Minimal
Hikable: Year-round
Map: Rambler's Guide to Trails of Mt. Tamalpais and the Marin Headlands, Olmsted & Brothers Map Company

Completed in 1873, this was the first reservoir built on the slopes of Mount Tamalpais. It is now the middle of three small lakes (Phoenix and Bon Tempe are the other two) on the lower slopes that are the center of popular hiking in the Marin Municipal Water District. Wildlife and wildflowers are both abundant here year-round, with something exciting going on all the time. Although the distance around this lake is short, there are enough interesting areas for it to be a half-day outing.

To reach Lagunitas and Bon Tempe lakes, take the Sir Francis Drake Boulevard exit off US 101, and continue to Fairfax. Turn left onto Broadway off Sir Francis Drake, go 1 block west, and turn left onto Bolinas Road. Continue for 1.5 miles to a white gate with a sign indicating Lagunitas and Bon Tempe lakes. Go through the gate and continue for 0.5 mile of winding road to the ranger station.

The north side of the lake is oak woodlands and grasslands that are relatively level, while on the south side a thick forest of redwoods and fir cover deep, moist ravines.

From the picnic area in the redwood grove near the base of the dam, where there is water and restrooms, the trail leads to the hooded spillway from the lake. In the winter and spring, after the rains, torrents of water overflow from the funnel of the spillway into a large pool. The water from the stream that flows from this pool pours into Bon Tempe Lake.

Stairs help you climb the trail to the top of the dam, where there is an excellent view of the 23-acre lake. In the 1980s a special aeration system was installed that controls the temperature and oxygen of the water in this lake in an attempt to help trout survive there year-round. After the system was installed, more than 9000 rainbow trout were stocked in the lake. Fish and game biologists hope that these stocked trout will become self-perpetuating, and that the lake will never again have to be

The lakes on the north slope of Mount Tamalpais are surrounded by scenic hiking trails.

stocked. These trout join a healthy population of large-mouth bass and blue gill that offer a challenge to fishermen and women of all ages.

Children also like the small wooden footbridges that cross the seasonal streams that bring water into Lagunitas about every 0.25 mile around the lake. These bridges can be used to drop leaves and sticks into when the streams are flowing strongly to watch them head to the lake, or as an access to the stream banks when the water is lower and moss-covered rocks are exposed. Many small animals and insects can be uncovered at that time.

For those wishing a little longer hike, the 3.5-mile loop of Bon Tempe Lake begins just to the west of the dam. The two loops together make a 5-mile hike.

Kent and Alpine lakes are the other two reservoirs in the district, and they both offer long and short hikes. Cataract Falls can be reached on a short 1-mile trail from a trailhead off the Bolinas-Fairfax Road near Alpine Dam, and Carson Falls above Kent Lake can be reached from the trailhead of Old Sled Trail that begins near Liberty Gulch on Alpine Lake.

13. Angel Island Trail Loop

Type: Dayhike
Difficulty: Moderate for children
Distance: 5 miles, loop
Hiking time: 4 hours
Elevation gain: Minimal
Hikable: Year-round
Map: USGS San Francisco North Topographic

This 1-square-mile island is the largest in San Francisco Bay and has a long history. In days past it has been a prison, an army fort, a missile base, and an immigration detention center. Today Angel Island State Park is a tranquil park in the midst of a bustling metropolitan region.

The native flora and fauna of the island are very similar to that of nearby mainland regions, but over the centuries humans have introduced a number of exotic plants. The state parks department has recently begun an effort to remove the large stands of exotic eucalyptus trees that have long been landmarks on the island. They are being removed because they are not native to the island, and the parks department has decided that they want to remove as many non-native trees from the island as they can to make it more like it was prior to human habitation.

The island is served by ferries from San Francisco (415-546-2896) and Tiburon (415-435-2131). Call for current schedules because they change seasonally.

The 5-mile loop trail that circles the island is relatively flat and passes through several historical sections. It begins at park headquarters near Ayala Cove, and it has both surfaced and nonsurfaced sections.

Take the road uphill from the headquarters for about 0.25 mile to Perimeter Road, which continues around the island. Various side trails lead hikers to historical sites, as well as vista points.

As you continue on Perimeter Road in a counterclockwise direction around the island, you will come to a number of historical sites. The first of these, at just over 1 mile, is Camp Reynolds, or the West Garrison. Established in 1863, this was the first military installation on the island. It was in continuous operation until 1946. A short side trail leads to the old buildings, which can be explored from the outside.

Bob and Mary Noyes have restored one of the buildings, and are living in it while they are supervising the restoration of others to the way they were in the 1880s. The buildings will be used for history programs once they are completely restored. Even now it is possible for children to imagine what life was like for soldiers during those years.

Return to the Perimeter Road and continue around the island. There is a spectacular view of San Francisco and the Golden Gate at 1.25 miles near an old gun emplacement, Battery Ledyard. Just past the emplacement a side trail leads off the main road for 0.25 mile down to small, sheltered Perles Beach. Children like to play in the sand here as they look for objects that have drifted ashore.

Continue on the Perimeter Road, which is now dirt, to just past 2 miles where there is a four-way junction. Take the road to the right, which becomes paved again, and after several hundred yards you are above Point Blunt, which was a favorite dueling grounds for San Franciscans in the 1800s. You overlook the point from an old Nike missile site that is not nearly as picturesque as Battery Ledyard, but still interesting historically.

The road goes downhill to about 2.5 miles, where it forks once again. Take the left fork, because the right one goes to a Coast Guard station that is off limits.

At 3 miles the road passes the East Garrison, which was built in the 1890s to house soldiers returning from the Philippines. This garrison is much less attractive and interesting than the West Garrison.

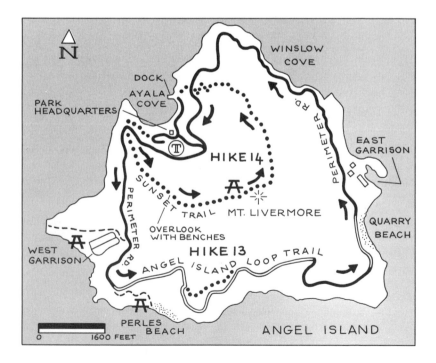

At 3.25 miles you overlook the North Garrison at Point Simpton, where an immigration station similar to Ellis Island in New York was established in 1909. There is a small museum on the history of the immigration station here that is well worth visiting. Children are intrigued by the stories of privations and challenges met by the early immigrants, most of whom were from Asia.

From the North Garrison return to the Perimeter Road and continue on past Point Campbell, the northernmost point of the island, at about 4 miles, and on back to Ayala Cove. At about 4.5 miles, the North Ridge Trail crosses Perimeter Road and heads down a series of stairs to the cove. This is a shorter, but steeper route back to the dock that you may choose. Otherwise continue on the road back to the cove.

In addition to the historical sites, seabirds and sea mammals are a primary attraction of this trail.

---

14. Sunset/North Ridge Trail Loop

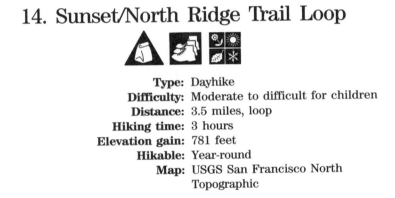

Type:	Dayhike
Difficulty:	Moderate to difficult for children
Distance:	3.5 miles, loop
Hiking time:	3 hours
Elevation gain:	781 feet
Hikable:	Year-round
Map:	USGS San Francisco North Topographic

To get a closeup view of the interior of Angel Island State Park and a panoramic view of San Francisco Bay, including the Golden Gate Bridge, the loop to the top of Mount Livermore is unexcelled. Raptors, seabirds, deer, and wildflowers all are attractions to this hike.

See information in hike 13, Angel Island Trail Loop, for access to Angel Island.

Begin by hiking to the Perimeter Road from the park headquarters and turn right. After about 0.5 mile, you'll see signs for Sunset Trail, which leads off to the left toward the center of the island.

Both portions of this loop were rerouted in 1990-91, making the ascent to the peak much easier. While the old trails were shorter, they were steeper, and distracted hikers from the surrounding beauty.

For the first 0.5 mile of the Sunset Trail you pass through a mixed bay and oak forest where there is plenty of evidence of deer, and it is

Angel Island trails offer views of the Marin Headlands.

not unusual to see one or more. If you do not see a deer, look instead for footprints along the trail and the ends of low branches that have been stripped off by hungry deer. On some trees and bushes, you can tell how tall the deer are by the height to which all the branches have been eaten.

Soon after you leave the canopy of this evergreen forest you reach a site with benches and a view of the Golden Gate Bridge and the hills of the Marin Headlands. Although early in the hike, it is well worth a short stop to enjoy the view. Although you will not have reached the summit at this point it is a good turnaround spot if the children are getting tired. If you go as far as the summit, it is actually easier to continue on rather than to turn back.

The trail continues toward the peak across open grassland, and at about 1 mile you reach the summit, where you will find water, picnic tables, and restrooms. The view from here encompasses all of San Francisco Bay, and since it is about halfway in your hike it makes an excellent lunch or snack break. To the south and east of the summit, you can see where large stands of eucalyptus have been removed, leaving scars that will take several years to disappear.

On the north side of the summit, take the North Ridge Trail, which descends through a mixed forest out into chaparral-covered hillsides. After about 0.5 mile, the trail curves above canyons filled with live oak and bay, while exotic Monterey pine give shade to the trail.

Near the end of the trail you begin a steep descent with steps and switchbacks, cross over the Perimeter Road, and climb down more steps to the rear of the snack bar.

15. Terwilliger Nature Trail Loop

Type: Dayhike
Difficulty: Easy for children
Distance: 0.5 mile, loop
Hiking time: About 1 hour
Elevation gain: Minimal
Hikable: Year-round
Map: USGS San Quentin Topographic

Richardson Bay Wildlife Sanctuary is operated by the Audubon Society as an environmental education center with a nature trail and interpretive programs for groups. It includes 11 acres of land and 900 acres of water with a variety of habitats for birds, small mammals, and other bayshore animals.

Take the Tiburon/Belvedere (CA-131) exit off US 101. Continue east on Tiburon Boulevard for about 1 mile, and turn right on Greenwood Cove Drive. This soon becomes Greenwood Beach Road. Follow this road for

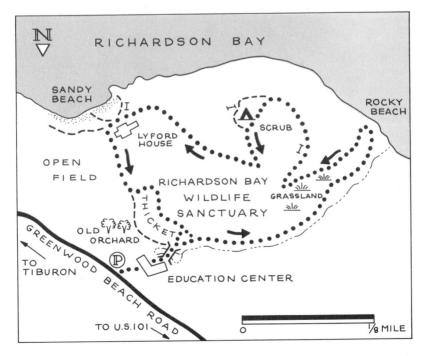

0.25 mile to the large yellow Victorian mansion on the right. Park by the education center off Greenwood Beach Road. The sanctuary is open 9:00 A.M. to 5:00 P.M., Wednesday–Sunday.

Pick up a self-guiding pamphlet at the education center. This gives an excellent introduction to the flora and fauna of the sanctuary as seen along the nature trail.

The trail begins behind the center and immediately crosses a small pond on a footbridge. Take the trail to the right along a seasonal creek for a short hike to Rocky Beach. There the trail loops back through some native grasses before it takes a sharp turn to the right. At about 0.25 mile there is a bench on the left of the trail from which you can relax and look out over the bay.

The Lyford House is a landmark of the Richardson Bay Wildlife Sanctuary.

Next along the trail you pass through some coastal scrub and head up a small hill where there is a good view of the San Francisco skyline across Richardson Bay.

The bird life here is very abundant and varied, so be sure to bring binoculars. Children can learn about some of the differences between how water birds and land birds live. Look for where the small land birds live and try to determine what they eat. Compare that with where the water birds live and what they eat.

Continue on the trail past the Lyford House, a lovingly restored Victorian mansion, and a thicket of impenetrable scrub that is home to hundreds of small birds, and on to the footbridge leading to the education center.

16. Corte Madera Ecological Reserve Trail

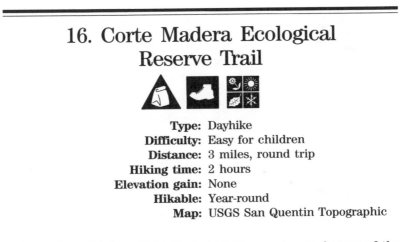

Type: Dayhike
Difficulty: Easy for children
Distance: 3 miles, round trip
Hiking time: 2 hours
Elevation gain: None
Hikable: Year-round
Map: USGS San Quentin Topographic

The Corte Madera State Ecological Reserve is one feature of the paved Corte Madera Creek Path that runs for 2 miles along Corte Madera Creek to San Francisco Bay. The reserve is a restored wetland and the creek is a wide, meandering creek that empties into the bay.

Take the Sir Francis Drake exit off US 101 and follow signs to the Golden Gate Ferry's Larkspur terminal. Park in the terminal parking lot.

From the terminal parking lot, head east on the path toward Remaillard Park, where the Marin Audubon Society has restored the duck pond and turtles and ducks can again be seen. Have the children search for turtles on small logs or other objects that stick up out of the water near taller water plants. They often can be seen warming themselves on sunny days, and you must be very quiet if you want to get a closeup look at them. You may also want to see how many different types of ducks are at the pond.

The Corte Madera Ecological Reserve is a pleasant break from the surrounding bustle of commerce.

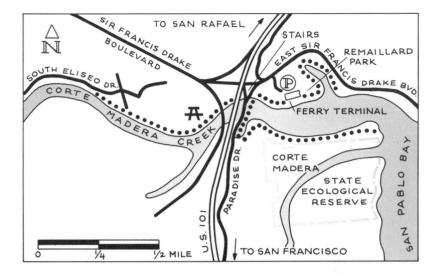

Circle around the pond on the dirt trail and head back to the parking lot the way you came. Continue past the parking lot and a group of false-fronted buildings just before the freeway. Just west on the path past the false-fronted buildings is a trail junction. To the left is the Corte Madera State Ecological Reserve.

To reach the reserve, leave the path and head left up the stairway to a sidewalk on the overpass. Follow Paradise Drive 0.5 mile to the reserve, then backtrack to the trail junction. Turn left under the freeway and out along the creek.

A small, grassy creekside park with picnic tables and benches located just past the freeway offers an excellent view of Mount Tamalpais as it towers over Corte Madera.

You can continue on the path along the creek for another 0.5 mile. Turn around at South Eliseo Drive and return to the ferry terminal parking lot.

17. Ridge Trail

Type: Dayhike
Difficulty: Easy to moderate for children
Distance: 2 miles, round trip
Hiking time: 2 hours
Elevation gain: 600 feet
Hikable: Year-round
Map: USGS San Quentin Topographic

Ring Mountain Preserve is a Nature Conservancy preserve that has been maintained in near pristine condition even though it is surrounded by development. It is home to seven rare plants, one of which grows nowhere else. Since these plants only grow in serpentine soil, which is found in very few places in the world but is the dominant soil on the ridge of the Tiburon Peninsula, their survival is dependent on the efforts of people such as those at the Nature Conservancy. The conservancy purchased the land that includes Ring Mountain to protect these delicate and tiny plants that few people in the world are able to see. Visitors to Ring Mountain Preserve, therefore, are among a privileged few to see such flowers as Tiburon buckwheat, Tiburon paintbrush, Marin dwarf flax, and black jewel flower (which grows only on the Tiburon Peninsula in serpentine soil) in bloom.

Take the Paradise Drive exit off US 101 in Corte Madera and follow the drive for a little over 1.5 miles to the entrance gate of the preserve, which will be on the right.

Wildflower fanciers flock to Ring Mountain from February through summer to view the many wildflowers that adorn the hillsides near the Ridge Trail, especially the lower slopes, and geologists come from all over the world to view the many types of schist that are found there.

The hike to the summit leads up an ancient landslide, and green serpentine dots the hillside. As you head up the trail between 0.25 mile and 0.75 mile have the children look for evidence of the ancient landslide (exposed rocks that appear to be left over from the slide or areas of soil that seem to lay at a different slope from the rest of the hillside).

They should also keep an eye out for some of the rare flowers, which are illustrated at the trailhead, during the spring. Stay on the trail and avoid walking on small plants. A level area at the top of the ridge was once the site of an antiaircraft installation, and now offers an ideal picnic site with views of large sections of the bay and surrounding hills.

Return to the trailhead by the same route.

Ring Mountain Preserve is full of color during spring bloom.

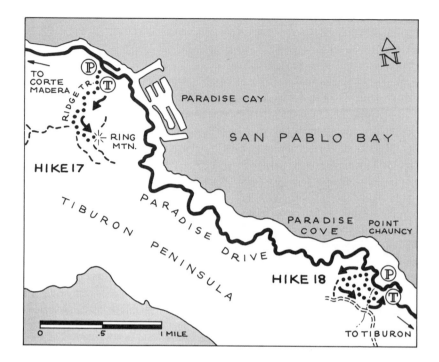

18. Tiburon Uplands Nature Preserve Trail Loop

Type: Dayhike
Difficulty: Moderate for children
Distance: 0.7 mile, loop
Hiking time: 1 hour
Elevation gain/loss: 300 feet
Hikable: Year-round
Map: USGS San Quentin

This 24-acre wooded nature preserve offers hikers an opportunity to explore one of the last undisturbed wooded uplands of the Tiburon Peninsula. It sits on the north side of the peninsula near the tip, is protected from the westerly winds, and receives considerable rainfall during the winter months. With the high rainfall, northern exposure, and lack of winds, the normally low-lying chaparral plants reach incredible sizes here. Toyon bushes normally have a center stem from 2 to 4 inches in diameter and reach a height of maybe 8 to 10 feet. However, along the first portion of the loop trail in the uplands preserve, Toyon grow to the size of small trees with trunks of up to 12 inches in diameter and reach a height of 18 to 20 feet. Several other chaparral plants grow to a similar size in the damp lower canyons. The same species are a more normal size on the more exposed upper slopes where the sun and winds dry out the soil.

Take the Paradise Drive exit off US 101 to Corte Madera and follow the drive past Paradise Beach Park. About 0.5 mile past the park, at just under 6 miles from the exit, San Francisco State University and the National Atmospheric and Oceanographic Administration have a center for ecological studies. Park in the gravel area just outside the gate to the center. Walk south along Paradise Drive around the curve. The trailhead for the preserve is across the road. Cross carefully because cars come around blind curves from both ways.

The trail begins above the steps beside the road. Take the trail to the right and head up the side of the dark canyon. For the first 0.25 mile, the trail switches back and forth as it climbs the canyon wall. It is along this stretch of trail that the chaparral plants grow to such large sizes. Point some of them out to the children on the hike and have them note how large they are.

By 0.3 mile, the trail has passed through the heaviest canopy of trees and shrubs and reached an airier and brighter location. Have the children look for smaller versions of chaparral plants along this section of the trail and compare the sizes with those from earlier on the trail.

At 0.3 mile a trail leads off to the right at a grass-covered knoll that offers good views of the Richmond/San Rafael Bridge to the north and the East Bay cities to the east. Many large oil tankers and cargo ships pass through the channel of the bay here, and children like to watch them as they pass under the bridge.

The trail to the right leads uphill to grass-covered slopes that are not part of the preserve, but are part of the Marin Parks and Open Space Department lands. This trail leads to the ridge above the town of Tiburon and offers views of the Marin Headlands and the Golden Gate. If you have energetic hikers who want to take a longer hike than the loop trail offers, take this side trail for up to 5 miles more of trails. If you do the side trip, return down the same trail to rejoin the loop trail.

After the trail junction above, the loop trail drops gently until about 0.5 mile. There it crosses a seasonal creek that can be a roaring torrent during the rainy season, as evidenced by the many large trees that have fallen into the canyon formed by the creek during high water. If the creek is too high it floods the trail and you will have to return to the trailhead by the same route you came.

A small patch of undisturbed nature is protected on the tip of the Tiburon Peninsula.

Generally there is no problem crossing the creek, though, and the trail takes a sharp left turn just past it as it begins its steep descent back to the trailhead.

At about 0.6 mile, the trail and creek flatten out as the canyon becomes much broader. Children can explore along the creek bed during dry times and climb on the many fallen trees that are scattered about.

This is a good place to rest and have a picnic if the ground is not too damp.

Continue back to the trailhead and return to the parking lot. Remember to watch for cars as you cross the road.

19. Deer Creek Trail Loop

Type: Dayhike
Difficulty: Easy for children
Distance: 0.75 mile, loop
Hiking time: 1 hour
Elevation gain: None
Hikable: Year-round
Map: USGS San Quentin Topographic

Deer Park is home to most species of Marin's native trees, including bay, buckeye, various oak, fir, and redwood. Although Deer Creek Trail Loop is short, it provides enough variety to conduct a full-fledged nature hike to introduce children to many of the natural communities of the region.

Take the Sir Francis Drake Boulevard exit off US 101 and continue to Fairfax. Turn left onto Broadway, go one block west, and turn left onto Fairfax-Bolinas Road. After a short distance turn left on Porteus Avenue. Continue on Porteus to the parking lot at Deer Park School.

Take the trail to the east out of the picnic area and head around

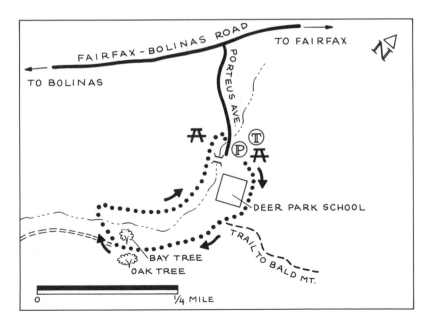

the school. This is the Deer Creek Trail Loop. Just past the school the trail takes a sharp turn to the left and heads to Bald Hill. Continue straight ahead to a gate and a fire road. This fire road takes you through a meadow for a little over 0.25 mile. There you will see an immense bay tree with a downed log underneath it. This is a good picnic or rest stop.

Across the fire road from the bay tree is a large oak tree with lichen hanging from its branches that children can explore under and around.

 Just past the bay tree the trail leads off to the right and crosses the creek, which you have to ford when it is high. It immediately turns to the right and follows the creek back to the parking lot. As you approach the school, there is a small grove of redwood trees next to the creek. Just past the redwood grove a small footbridge takes you back across the creek to the parking lot.

There are picnic areas on both sides of the creek near the school parking lot.

Deer Creek Trail is used by all age groups, and rest stops are important.

20. Miller Creek Trail

Type: Dayhike
Difficulty: Easy for children
Distance: 0.75 mile, loop
Hiking time: 1 hour
Elevation gain: None
Hikable: Year-round
Map: USGS San Quentin Topographic

This trail explores a bit of wilderness along an undisturbed creek in Marinwood at the Old Dixie School Community Park. The area is thick with a variety of trees, including bay, willow, buckeye, oak, and alder, and many types of small wildlife can be observed there.

Take the Lucas Valley Road exit off US 101 and go west for about 0.5 mile. Turn north on Las Gallinas Avenue to the parking lot at the Old Dixie Schoolhouse.

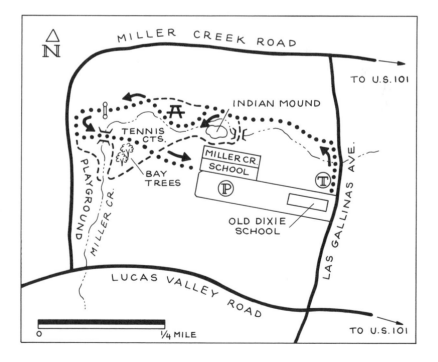

Miller Creek Park offers picnicking opportunities under broad canopied bay trees.

From the parking lot take the asphalt walkway north of the old schoolhouse over Miller Creek. Turn left on the dirt trail and follow along the creek. At about 0.2 mile, a trail splits off to the left to follow the creek. Take this trail along the creek for several hundred feet. As it rejoins the original trail there is a large bay tree with a picnic area underneath. The tree is scarred, has broken limbs, and is hollowed out inside, but still survives. While you take a break underneath the tree, have the children explore the scars and try to figure out how it can still be alive with all the damage to it. (The nourishment to the limbs and leaves of a tree reaches them through a thin layer of cells called the cambrian layer. This layer is between the bark and the heartwood of a tree, and is the slick, wet substance that can be felt and seen as bark is peeled from a live limb or tree. A tree can survive as long as some portion of this layer is left uninterrupted between the roots and the leaves. Since this old bay still has some portion of its cambrian layer it can survive.)

Continue on the trail for a short distance to the footbridge that crosses the creek toward the new Miller Creek School. Just over the creek is an old Indian mound that was excavated in the 1960s. The site is estimated to have been occupied by the Coast Miwok for at least 3000 years.

Follow the trail from the mound toward the bay forest, and circle the forest before looping back to the parking lot.

21. Pickleweed Marsh Trail

Type: Dayhike
Difficulty: Easy for children
Distance: 1 to 1.5 miles, loop
Hiking time: 1 hour
Elevation gain: None
Hikable: Year-round
Map: USGS San Quentin Topographic

China Camp State Park is a 1500-acre preserve on Point San Pedro Peninsula near San Rafael. A thriving shrimp-fishing village was located on the tip of the peninsula in the last century, but now only a few buildings remain. These are part of the state park, and most park visitors stay close to the village to enjoy the protected beach and relatively warm water. This leaves the majority of the 1500 acres uncrowded, even on weekends, and numerous trails lead into the various natural communities found in the park.

Take the Central San Rafael exit past the Civic Center to North San Pedro Road. Head east through a residential section of town to the park. You can park at one of the pullouts near Turtle Back, or at the Back

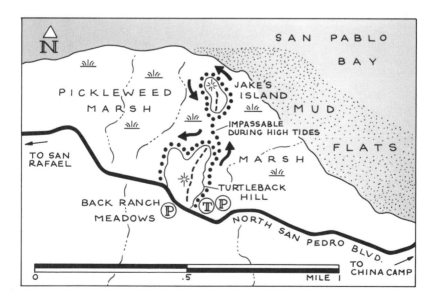

Ranch Meadows parking lot. The latter requires a day-use fee, however.

This 1-mile-long trail encircles Turtle Back, and is a self-guided nature trail that leads you past a saltwater marsh and scrub-covered hills on the south side. At about 0.5 mile a trail leads out to Jake's Island, which is easily accessible if the tide is out, but which is separated from the rest of the trail when the tide is high. (A side trip to Jake's Island would be a good way to have a picnic in solitude on most days, and you get good views of the marshes surrounding the island. Bird watching is good here year-round.)

It is best to check the local tide table before planning a picnic on the island, but if you happen to be out on the island when the tide begins to come in, you can easily return to the trail around Turtle Back since the tides in this section of the bay are not large, and the water separating Jake's Island and Turtle Back seldom gets more than a foot deep.

If you take this hike on a day when Jake's Island is accessible, there are a number of potholes in the marsh around sloughs and rocks near the island that have small crabs and other small sea animals that can be readily observed when the water is low. Children like to watch the crabs come out from beneath rocks and overhangs to feed and then scurry back in when shadows fall on them. If the route around Jake's Island is not available, have the children watch for the dramatic change in vegetation types as they round Turtle Back from the south to the north.

Jake's Island, unreachable at high tide, is accessible during low tide.

Interpretive plaques are located at various spots along the trail explaining why the vegetation changes as it does.

As you pass the trail to Jake's Island, and go around to the north side of Turtle Back, the growth on the hillsides changes from scrub to oak and bay forests complete with ferns and green undergrowth. The shade provided by the hill provides just enough more moisture to allow this change.

As you near the end of the trail, the shade gives way to the heat and dryness of a southern exposure, and the flora once again changes, this time to madrone, manzanita, and live oak.

22. Back Ranch/Ridge Trail Loop

Type:	Dayhike
Difficulty:	Difficult for children
Distance:	5 miles, loop
Hiking time:	3 hours
Elevation gain:	1000 feet
Hikable:	Year-round
Map:	USGS San Quentin Topographic

This hike in China Camp State Park leads you away from the marshlands of the bay and into the steep hills. These are covered by forests of bay, oak, and madrone on the lower slopes, and fir and oak higher up. On the most exposed higher slopes, manzanita, coyote brush, and toyon form a brushy cover.

Follow the directions for hike 21, Pickleweed Marsh Trail, to the trailhead, which is across the road from Turtle Back.

The trail begins in an open grassy meadow and wanders back to the campground area, with only an occasional valley oak in the meadow. Heavier woods begin near the campground and continue along the creek up the trail. The first mile of the trail is steep, and you soon encounter a number of challenging switchbacks that are difficult for most children under eight years of age. These gradually disappear, and at about 1.5 miles the Back Ranch Meadows Trail dead ends into the Ridge Trail. At this point you can either turn right for about 0.5 mile to a delightful picnic spot and view an old Nike missile site, or turn left onto the Ridge Trail. The trail to the missile site is uphill, but the view you have while taking a lunch or snack break is well worth the extra effort. Children

A hike is a good time for children to enjoy their grandparents.

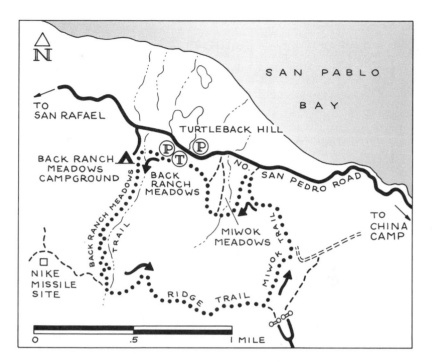

like to watch the many boats that cross the waters of the bay. See how many sailboats, ferries, tankers, and other types they can spot. This is also a good spot to watch for large soaring birds such as hawks and vultures. Try to show the children how to tell them apart from a distance. (Vultures soar with their wings up in a V, while hawks keep their wings level.)

After your break, you may return on the Back Ranch Meadows Trail for a roundtrip of 4 miles, or take the Ridge Trail and begin a slow descent for about 0.75 mile, where the trail divides. Take the left fork for about another 0.25 mile, where the Miwok Trail joins the Ridge Trail.

Follow the steep descent of the Miwok Trail back toward Miwok Meadows and out of the shelter of the forest. The trail takes a sharp left turn just before you reach the road, circles around Miwok Meadows and the group day-use area, and crosses more grassland for about 0.25 mile to the trailhead.

23. Rat Rock Cove Trail

Type: Dayhike
Difficulty: Easy for children
Distance: 1 mile, round trip
Hiking time: 1 hour
Elevation gain: 100 feet
Hikable: Year-round
Map: USGS San Quentin Topographic

China Camp State Park has a large beach to the south of the historic area that is a popular swimming and sunbathing area, but just north of the parking and picnic area on China Camp Point there is another small beach that offers hikers an opportunity to explore a small marsh, play on the beach, and birdwatch near Five Pine Point.

Follow the directions in hike 21, Pickleweed Marsh Trail, to China Camp State Park, but continue on North San Pedro Road for about 1 additional mile past Turtle Back to China Camp Point and the historic area. The trail to Rat Rock Cove heads north from the parking lot and picnic area.

Before the trail reaches the beach at about 0.3 mile, it passes through a small segment of saltwater marsh, complete with a side trail around a pond area. This is a good place to investigate and many small marsh plants and animals can be observed here.

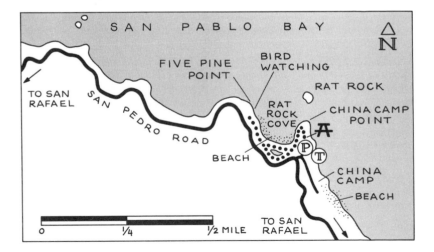

The beach is small, but large enough for the kids to enjoy building sandcastles and playing in the gentle waves.

The trail ends at Five Pine Point, which is a good spot to watch shorebirds, especially when the tide is out.

Low-lying trees offer good protection for picnickers during warm days.

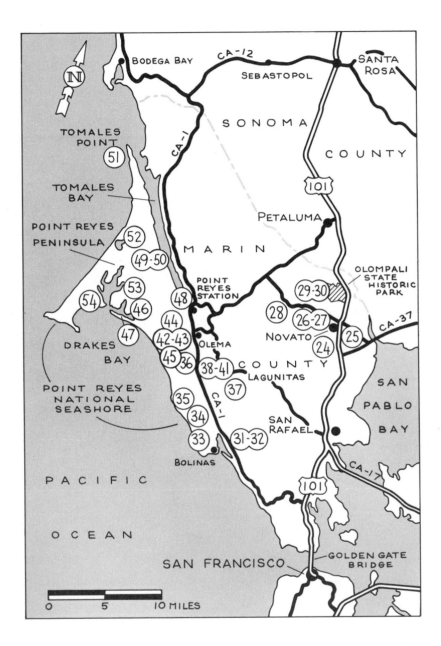

Northern/Western Marin

A visual joy can be found in every small pond.

Scottsdale Pond was saved by the citizens of Novato for the enjoyment of all.

24. Scottsdale Pond Trail Loop

Type: Dayhike
Difficulty: Easy for children
Distance: 1 mile, loop
Hiking time: 1 hour
Elevation gain: None
Hikable: Year-round
Map: USGS Petaluma Topographic

Scottsdale Pond, a small freshwater lagoon, is easily overlooked as you speed by on the freeway, but the people of Novato decided it was worth preserving, and it has become an excellent example of environmental conservation. It is a resting area for many migrating waterfowl, and is a sensitive natural habitat that is home to many small mammals and numerous birds.

Take the Rowland Boulevard exit off US 101 in Novato, and turn left on Redwood Boulevard just west of the freeway. The lagoon is on your left just south of Rowland, and plenty of parking is available.

This is a good place to take a short hike to watch birds, picnic, or simply enjoy a sunny outing around water. There is no definite trail, but plenty of use has made an easily passable path that circles the pond.

Midwinter hikes here are rewarding since so many migrating water-

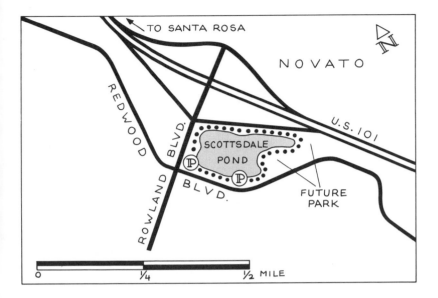

fowl can be seen, including geese, swans, and ducks from mudhens to mallards.

Bring some stale bread or other bird feed for the kids to feed the fowl and you will be able to view the birds up close!

25. Deer Island Trail Loop

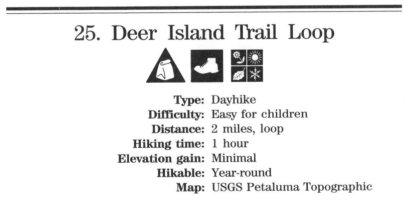

Type: Dayhike
Difficulty: Easy for children
Distance: 2 miles, loop
Hiking time: 1 hour
Elevation gain: Minimal
Hikable: Year-round
Map: USGS Petaluma Topographic

This small hill was once an island surrounded by San Francisco Bay, but today stands as a sentinel in the marshlands east of Novato that were formed as the wetlands were drained and filled. Today signs of deer, raccoon, rabbit, skunk, fox, and bobcat can all be observed on a walk around the hill.

Every dead snag is home to a wide variety of wildlife.

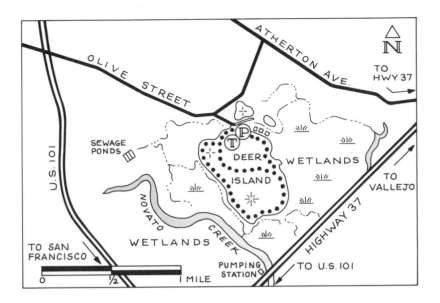

Take the Atherton Avenue exit off US 101 and head east to Olive Avenue. Turn right on Olive and then left on Deer Island Lane. There is parking near the hill.

The trail is an easy walk around the hill, and a wide variety of wildflowers can be seen on the slopes of the hill during the spring. About half the island is covered by huge bay and oak trees that have stood for hundreds of years. The other half is open grassland.

The Novato water treatment plant can be seen to the southeast of the hill, and Novato Creek's levees are to the southwest. This low-lying area is an important resting area and breeding ground for birds.

There are actually two trails on the hill. The first circles the base, and the second, which branches off the first near the parking area, leads to the top of the hill, and then makes a short loop back to the outer trail. Both trails offer a variety of views, and neither is strenuous.

Since it is almost impossible to get lost on this hike, the children may want to take the trail that leads to the top of the hill and hike down the other side of the island to meet those who want to hike around the perimeter of the island.

26. Miwok Trail

Type:	Dayhike
Difficulty:	Easy for children
Distance:	0.5 mile, loop
Hiking time:	45 minutes
Elevation gain:	Minimal
Hikable:	Year-round
Map:	USGS Petaluma Topographic

The main feature of Miwok Park is the Miwok Museum, but the nature walk along the Miwok Trail comes in a close second. Although relatively short it is an enjoyable outing with young children. The trail leads along the meandering Novato Creek, crosses a footbridge, and heads up a small hill covered with live oak.

Streams add to the enjoyment of North Bay walks.

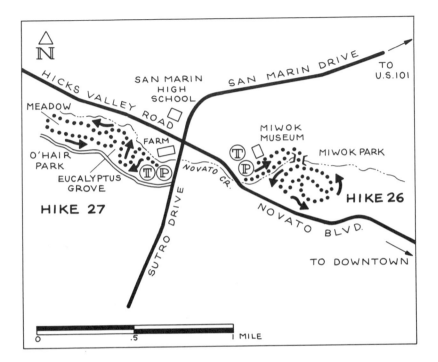

Take the Delong exit in Novato off US 101, and head west to Business
101. Make a left turn onto Business 101 and a right on Diablo Avenue
to Novato Boulevard. Miwok Park is located about 1.5 miles farther on
Novato Boulevard. Parking is available on the right just past Novato Creek.

A small grove of redwood trees was planted near the parking lot
when the park was developed. An asphalt walk begins at the parking lot
and heads past the museum. When it dead ends, take a right back toward
Novato Boulevard. As the walkway approaches the road a trail heads back
up the creek for several hundred yards. This section takes you along the
creek. Watch for signs of deer and raccoon since they come here for
water: their hoof- and footprints. Also, the deer browse on low branches
of trees, stripping them of their leaves.

The trail rejoins the walkway for a short distance just past the picnic
area, and then crosses the creek by a footbridge. From there it winds
up to the summit of the small hill. About halfway to the top a trail leads
off to the left and bypasses the summit to rejoin the main trail near the
archery range.

From the summit you can see the valley below that is filled with
homes, and the unpopulated Big Rock Ridge to the south.

The trail descends from the summit and returns to the footbridge,
where you head back to the museum area.

27. Trail Loop

Type: Dayhike
Difficulty: Easy for children
Distance: 1 mile, loop
Hiking time: 1 hour
Elevation gain: Minimal
Hikable: Year-round
Map: USGS Petaluma Topographic

O'Hair Park is an undeveloped park on the northwest side of Novato that has a creek and a meadow of native grasses. In the summer the creek is stocked with trout and becomes a favorite fishing spot for Novato youth. The fish also attract belted kingfishers, a diving bird that sits on branches above the creek and dives down to catch fish that venture near the surface.

Take the Atherton Avenue exit off US 101 and head west. Atherton Avenue turns into San Marin Drive just west of the freeway. Continue west on San Marin Drive to Hicks Valley Road, which is just past San Marin High School. San Marin Drive becomes Sutro Avenue after it crosses Hicks Valley Road, and parking for O'Hair Park is on the right side of the road just after you cross Novato Creek. The trail begins near the creek at the north end of the parking area.

Many small animals and birds, plus deer, frequent the creek area and live in and around the bay and oak trees that grow on the banks of the creek. The blackberry brambles that grow along the edges of the trees also provide protection and food for birds, raccoons, skunks, opossums, and squirrels.

The trail follows along the creek bank for about 0.25 mile before it turns toward a fire road that leads from the southern end of the parking area. Follow the fire road for about 100 yards, where the trail leads off to the right toward a large stand of eucalyptus trees. These exotic trees were planted as wind breaks and boundary markers by early settlers.

Just past the stand of eucalyptus the trail branches into four directions. The left branch heads up a small hill that overlooks the meadow; the left-center branch leads straight through the middle of the meadow, and the right-center leads around the right side of the meadow. The far right branch is a small loop that leads along the edge of the eucalyptus grove down to the creek before circling back to join the right-center branch in the meadow.

The right-center and far right branches give the best introduction

Even vultures enjoy sunny winter mornings.

to the meadow, and lead you through native bunch grasses of the types that once covered most of California. Today these grasses, which can reach as high as 5 feet, only grow in small areas widely scattered around the state. They are noticeably different from the now common introduced grasses that generally do not exceed 2 feet in height.

Near the far end of the meadow, at around 0.5 mile, there is a large, old bay tree with large hollow cavities that many animals use as home. These sometimes even harbor small water animals because they fill up during winter rains. This is a good site for a picnic, and the kids will enjoy examining the holes for signs of activity.

The rest of the hike takes you up a small hill where you overlook the meadow and then leads back to the eucalyptus grove. From there you can head back to the parking lot, either along the fire road or the creekside trail.

Marshes dry up during drought years, only to return as the rains come.

28. Nature Trail Loop

Type:	Dayhike
Difficulty:	Moderate for children
Distance:	2.5 miles, loop
Hiking time:	3 hours
Elevation gain:	200 feet
Hikable:	Year-round
Map:	USGS Petaluma Topographic

Stafford Lake is a reservoir on Novato Creek, and the county park that surrounds it includes marshlands and riparian habitats that are home to a wide variety of wildlife. There are also oak woodlands and open grasslands along the hike to an overlook that offers views of the lake and surrounding ridges.

 Take the Novato Boulevard exit off US 101 and head west. Continue for a little over 6 miles to the sign for Stafford Lake County Park. After entering the parking area, turn right and go to the end for the trailhead.

The trail leads upstream away from the lake between the creek and a fence. After about 0.25 mile, the trail leads through a gate, and almost immediately to the left is a series of four footbridges that cross over a marshy area with cattails and rushes. Flocks of blackbirds live here, as well as hundreds of frogs that frequently float on the surface of the water.

The trail goes through another gate just after the marsh and, immediately after passing the junction of the Nature Trail coming in on the left and a fire road on the right, begins a series of switchbacks uphill through open grassland and scattered oaks. Colorful wildflowers cover both sides of this stretch of trail from late February until June, and families of California quail can often be seen scattering at the approach of hikers.

At about 1 mile there is a trail junction. You will find a rest area to the left of the trail just downhill from the junction, but scenic views are better observed by continuing uphill for another 0.25 mile after the junction. There is a good view at the second switchback past the junction just before you reach a grove of redwood trees that all have their tops broken off at the same height. Can the kids guess how this damage happened? (It was probably caused by a strong windstorm sometime in the past, and side branches have begun to climb upward to replace the lost tops.)

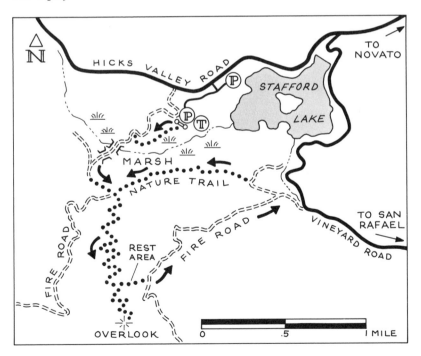

The trail ends at an overlook about 100 yards past the redwood grove, and this is an excellent place for a picnic or snack break. This view of the hills and ravines around the lake shows where water accumulates in the valleys to help support many shrubs and trees. Only annual grasses and wildflowers grow on the open hillsides, which become extremely dry after the rains stop in the spring.

Return down the trail to the junction, and turn right to complete a loop back to the marsh area. The trail deadends into a fire road about 100 yards after the junction. Turn left onto the fire road to continue downhill. This portion of the trail leads through open grassland with few trees (although there is one with a bench beneath it about 0.25 mile from the trail junction), and wildflowers grow in abundance during the spring.

The fire road deadends into another just before 2 miles. Take a left at the junction and follow the second fire road for about 200 yards. At that point it takes a sharp right, and the Nature Trail leads off to the left. Take the Nature Trail across the meadow to about 2.25 miles, where it joins with the main trail. Turn right on the main trail to head back to the trailhead.

There are picnic areas near the parking lot where you can rest after the hike.

29. Reservoir Trail Loop

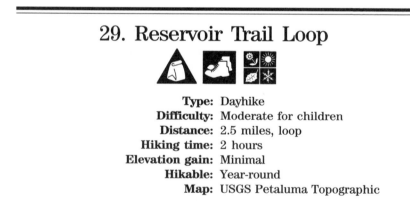

Type: Dayhike
Difficulty: Moderate for children
Distance: 2.5 miles, loop
Hiking time: 2 hours
Elevation gain: Minimal
Hikable: Year-round
Map: USGS Petaluma Topographic

Olompali State Historic Park is one of the newer state park units in the North Bay, and it has both historical and natural features that make it a worthwhile visit. The site was used by Native Americans for hundreds of years for a large village, and it is even debated that Sir Francis Drake may have visited because a silver sixpence coin was uncovered during an excavation in 1974. It includes Burdell Mountain, one of the highest spots in northern Marin County, and pleasant short hikes near the historic area.

The park is located on the west side of US 101 north of Novato. Entry

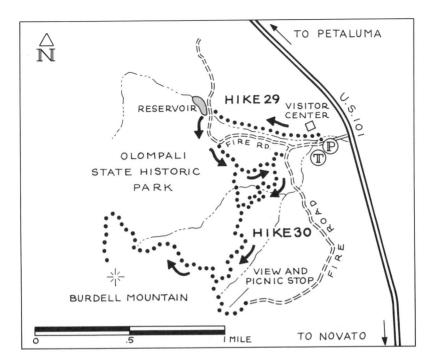

into the park is simple for those heading south; the entrance is well marked and requires only a right turn off the freeway. Those heading north, however, must continue past the park for about 2.5 miles to the San Antonio Road exit off US 101. Instead of turning left onto San Antonio, use the exit to make a U-turn, which is legal at this particular turn. Head back south to the park entrance.

From the rear of the parking lot, follow the gravel road north. It takes you along a pomegranate hedge that protects the remains of a once spectacular formal garden. The hedge is full of pink and white flowers during the spring. The pomegranates seldom produce fruit in this climate, but if they do happen to have fruit, they should not be picked.

You soon cross a bridge to the north side of the creek and turn left along a fire road. At about 0.5 mile, you cross back over the creek. On your right is a small reservoir and several concrete basins that were once used to water the magnificent gardens of the estate. Children will enjoy exploring around the edges of these basins for small water animals that live in the moss and algae that grow there.

You can return to the parking lot from here for a short 1-mile loop, but most will prefer to continue on the fire road past the reservoir, and then turn left on a new trail heading up the side of the ravine.

This trail takes you uphill through areas shaded by oak, bay, and madrone, and joins the trail to the top of Burdell Mountain at about 0.75 mile. Veer to your left and continue on the trail for another 0.25 mile. The trail crosses the creek there, and this is a good spot to take a snack or picnic break.

A short distance past the creek the trail begins a fairly steep descent, and includes many switchbacks as it heads back to the parking lot. It alternately leads through shaded forest and open grassland, both of which have many wildflowers in the spring.

Oaks are a pleasure to look at during any season.

30. Burdell Mountain Summit Trail

Type: Dayhike
Difficulty: Difficult for children
Distance: 6 miles, round trip
Hiking time: 5 hours
Elevation gain: 1500 feet
Hikable: Year-round
Map: USGS Petaluma Topographic

Although the emphasis at Olompali State Historic Park is on the historical significance of the site, which has been inhabited by Native Americans or Europeans for more than 500 years, there is much more to be explored. The park includes over 700 acres, and in the midst of that is 1558-foot Burdell Mountain, which offers panoramic views of the Petaluma River as it meanders toward San Pablo Bay and of northern Marin County. The slopes of the steep ravines formed by the many seasonal creeks that drain the eastern side of Burdell Mountain are covered with forests of oak, bay, and madrone, and are home to many animals. Deer are plentiful here, and signs of coyote and bobcat are often seen. Wildflowers are profuse in the open grasslands and the less dense areas of the forest from early spring to June.

Follow the directions for hike 29, Reservoir Trail Loop, to reach the park. From the parking lot, take the fire road that turns left uphill to begin the trip to the summit.

The first 0.5 mile of the trail goes through sparsely forested grassland, and several large bay trees are found on both sides of the trail. At just under 0.5 mile, a trail leads off the fire road to the right. Take this to continue to the summit. The forest almost immediately becomes denser, and good groves of madrone soon appear.

The trail winds up the side of a steep ravine, and at about 1.5 miles passes a large manzanita on the right and curves sharply to the right to cross the head of the ravine. Straight ahead there is a saddle in the ridge and a small hill to the left. This is a good place to take a break and have lunch. The view of the marshlands is good here, although not as spectacular as from the summit.

The manzanita is a close relative of the madrone trees that become more numerous on the next stretch of the trail. Have the children feel the smooth bark of the large manzanita, look at its leaves, and maybe even taste its small fruit. (Manzanita means "small apple" in Spanish. See if the children can figure out why the plant was named this.) They

Large trees are a good rest stop—children love to climb on them.

can compare what they found with one of the large madrones near the trail farther on, and discuss the similarities and differences of the two trees.

 If it appears that the trek to the summit is beyond the capacity of your little ones, this is a good turnaround spot. As I was hiking the trail for this guidebook, a new branch was being developed that heads south from this site; it will form a loop that returns to the parking lot. This loop is about 3 miles total.

For those who continue to the summit, the trail crosses the ridge and follows the contours of another, larger ravine. The madrone become both more numerous and larger at this point.

At about 2 miles the forest thins out for about 0.5 mile and you go through some scrub growth before reentering a forested area. This area contains large fir as well as oak and bay, and the pass crosses some very steep slopes.

After leaving the fir forest the trail continues steeply uphill, crosses the headwaters of a large creek, and winds around to the peak of Burdell Mountain.

The return trip to the parking lot is easy because it is completely downhill, although some of the steeper stretches can put a strain on your knees if you attempt to travel too fast.

31. Rawlings/Kent Trail Loop

Type: Dayhike
Difficulty: Moderate for children
Distance: 1 mile, loop
Hiking time: 1 hour
Elevation gain: 250 feet
Hikable: March-July
Map: USGS Bolinas Topographic

Great blue herons and great egrets are wonderfully colorful birds that are often seen individually around the bay area, but they can be seen at their finest each spring at the Audubon Canyon Ranch near Bolinas Lagoon. The great blue heron stands 4 to 5 feet tall, and has a wingspan of up to 6 feet. The great egret is only slightly smaller and has outstanding breeding plumage. This plumage almost caused the extinction of the birds during the early part of the twentieth century as

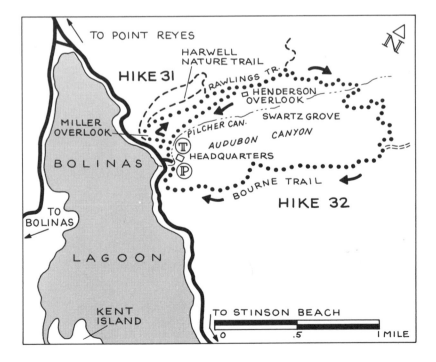

Waterfowl can be found in most of the lakes and marshes of the North Bay.

hunters killed them by the thousands for their beautiful feathers, which were used as ornaments for women's hats. Both of these magnificent birds build their nest of sticks high in redwood trees in a large rookery in Picher Canyon behind the headquarters of Audubon Canyon Ranch, where they can be viewed from an overlook during breeding season. The birds are protected in the redwood forest, and they have a ready supply of food in nearby Bolinas Lagoon.

Take the Stinson Beach exit from US 101, and continue on CA-1 for 3.25 miles past Stinson Beach. Signs on the right side of the highway lead you to the parking lot at headquarters. The trail to the overlook heads uphill behind the visitor center.

The Rawlings Trail heads up the side of a ravine to the north of the visitor center, then heads through a heavily forested area with a canopy of oak, bay, and madrone. During the spring this part of the trail has many wildflowers and mushrooms.

At the first sharp U-turn at about 0.2 mile, you will find an overlook named after the late congressman Clem Miller. From this overlook you can watch herons, egrets, and other birds fishing in Bolinas Lagoon while resting on a bench.

At about 0.5 mile you come to the Henderson Overlook, where you are at a slightly higher elevation than the nests in the Picher Canyon rookery. There are a number of wooden benches at the overlook where you can sit and watch the constant activity of over 120 herons and egrets as they fly from their nests to the lagoon and back. The herons begin nesting in late February and the egrets several weeks later in March. Between mid-April and mid-June the rookery is especially exciting as several hundred nestlings are hatched and squawking for food.

After you have seen enough of the herons and egrets return the 0.5 mile to the visitor center on the slightly steeper Kent Trail.

You may wish to pick up the leaflet to the Bert C. Harwell Nature Trail, a 1-mile loop that is just north of the Rawlings/Kent Trail Loop, and add a hike along it to this one.

Audubon Canyon Ranch is only open to visitors during the nesting season, generally March through July, and then only on Saturdays, Sundays, and holidays from 10:00 A.M. to 4:00 P.M.

32. Griffin/Borne Trail Loop

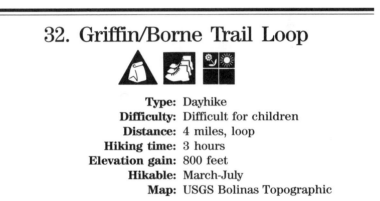

Type:	Dayhike
Difficulty:	Difficult for children
Distance:	4 miles, loop
Hiking time:	3 hours
Elevation gain:	800 feet
Hikable:	March-July
Map:	USGS Bolinas Topographic

For those who wish to have a little more strenuous hike after viewing the rookery (hike 31), Audubon Canyon Ranch has developed several longer trails that lead through the forests and grasslands of the preserve. All of this land has been defended against various intrusions since the 1960s. Developers attempted to subdivide the area, loggers wanted to denude the ravines of redwoods, and others wanted to widen the highway or build marinas near what is now the preserve. Finally, a great oil spill in 1971 threatened to destroy the fisheries and feeding grounds of Bolinas Lagoon, but thousands of volunteers fought to keep all of these threats from infringing on the natural beauty of the area and raised money to buy the canyonlands in the present preserve, as well as Kent Island. Today the area is open for exploring and hiking from March to July.

See hike 31, Rawlings/Kent Trail Loop, for directions to preserve. Begin this loop by heading up Rawlings Trail to the Henderson Overlook as you did in hike 31.

From the overlook, Griffin Trail climbs fairly steeply through a forest of bay, oak, and buckeye, and leads through a variety of wildflowers from March through May. The trail levels off about 1 mile past the overlook (1.5 miles from the trailhead). It then reaches the head of Picher Canyon where the creek rushes down the canyon through ferns and horsetails. There is a bench near the creek where you can rest and enjoy the quiet solitude of the redwood grove.

Have the children look for different kinds of ferns along the creek, and see if they can find spores underneath any fern leaves. Children can feel the silica in the ridges along the stalk of the horsetails. Silica is rough like grains of sand and the horsetail stalks are Nature's "nail files." This prehistoric plant was used as scrub brushes by Native Americans, and one local name for it is Indian scrub brush.

For the next 0.5 mile, the trail follows the contour of the south side of the ravine through redwoods and bay. You leave the canopy of the forest, climb a short distance through chaparral, and come to an overlook that offers a view of Bolinas Lagoon.

The trail soon merges with the Bourne Trail, which comes in from the left, and heads downhill through open grassland toward the ranch headquarters. The view from this section of the trail includes a panorama from Stinson Beach to the south to the Point Reyes Peninsula to the north.

Many birds can be seen along the trail here (over 60 species of land birds live here year-round), as well as wildflowers.

The trail curves into a grove of coast live oak just before it reaches the Audubon headquarters, where you can enjoy a restful picnic or explore the exhibits and bookstore.

It is wise to let small wildlife enjoy the fruits of the mushroom, since many are extremely poisonous to humans.

The reefs off Agate Beach are fully covered during high tide.

33. Agate Beach Trail

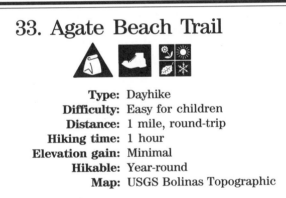

Type: Dayhike
Difficulty: Easy for children
Distance: 1 mile, round-trip
Hiking time: 1 hour
Elevation gain: Minimal
Hikable: Year-round
Map: USGS Bolinas Topographic

There are a number of excellent beach walks in the North Bay region, but Agate Beach, part of the Marin County Parks Department, is one of the most varied. When the tide is out, there are extensive tide pools in a reef that is just offshore, and when the tide is in, the pebbles that cover the beach offer hikers a chance to rest and explore.

Take the road to Bolinas off CA-1 just north of Bolinas Lagoon. Turn right on Mesa Road, go about 1 mile to Overlook, and make a left. Turn right on Elm and continue for about 1.5 miles to the Agate Beach Public Fishing Access. Signs direct you to the beach from the parking lot.

As with most beach walks there are no marked trails, and hikes take a more free-form approach. At Agate children like to explore the tide pools, run along the long beach, and search for small agates found among the small pebbles that cover the beach. This short hike is easy for beginners, and in addition to the above activities, everyone can observe birds along the shore.

34. Fern Canyon Trail

Type: Dayhike
Difficulty: Moderate for children
Distance: 1 mile, loop
Hiking time: 1 hour
Elevation gain: 200 feet
Hikable: Year-round
Map: Erickson's Map of
Point Reyes National
Seashore, Tomales Bay, and
Taylor State Parks

Point Reyes National Seashore is an outstanding example of how large tracts of near-virgin land can be set aside near major metropolitan areas for the enjoyment of all. It contains thousands of acres of untamed wilderness and features hundreds of hikes. At the southern end of the seashore is a little-known canyon of the Arroyo Hondo Creek, which drains an 8-mile-long, 8000-acre watershed. The creek runs year-round and provides the canyon with enough water to form an almost tropical ecological system. With native rainbow trout, giant salamanders, rough-skinned newts, a dozen resident bird species, and four major types of ferns, there is plenty of flora and fauna for all.

Take the Stinson Beach exit off US 101. Head north on CA-1 for 4.5 miles past Stinson Beach. At the north end of Bolinas Lagoon, CA-1 is joined by Bolinas-Fairfax Road (this may not be marked). Turn left onto this road and follow it for 1.25 miles on the west side of Bolinas Lagoon to Mesa Road. Turn right on Mesa and continue for about 4 miles. This takes you into the Point Reyes National Seashore, past the U.S. Coast Guard Station, and to the Palomarin Field Station of the Point Reyes Bird Observatory. Park in the lot just beyond the field station building. The Fern Canyon trailhead begins on the east side of the parking lot.

Bird banding occurs at the field station during various seasons, and a small museum at the field station describes the activities that take place there. Ornithologists are people who study birds. They study migration by catching birds, placing a small, colored band with information about who placed the band around one leg, and then releasing them. If these birds are later recaptured by other ornithologists, or found by nonscientists, the person who banded the bird is notified. This gives scientists much information about where and when birds travel. Children can observe birds being banded at the field station, and families can actually help with the banding by volunteering in advance.

Ferns grow profusely in the cool, shaded environments of evergreen forests.

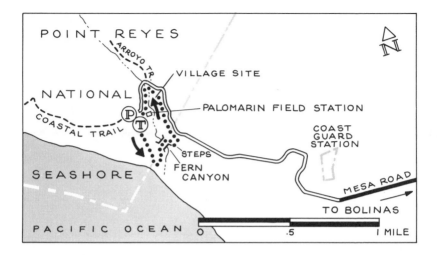

A small leaflet, titled *Fern Canyon Guide,* can also be picked up at the field station. This guide is not a "go-by-the-numbers" guide, but has drawings of animals, birds, plants, and landscapes, along with written descriptions, to help you locate your position on the nature trail. Have the children use the guide to keep track of where you are.

The first part of the trail descends gently through coastal scrub, which is dotted by poles that mark study grids used by the field station.

At about 0.25 mile, the trail comes to an overlook above the edge of the woodland that covers most of Fern Canyon. The overlook is well used and is the only spot where you should leave the main trail. Any side trails you encounter are for the use of field station researchers.

Just past the overlook the trail plunges down into the dark recesses of the canyon. There a canopy of evergreens such as bay and oak shade the creekside and provide a glen where five-finger, polypody, lady, and sword ferns abound.

To reach the glen, which is about 0.5 mile from the trailhead, you must descend a four-rung ladder. Stop and explore the many wonders to be found in such enchanted places.

To begin the final leg of the hike, you cross the creek on a footbridge and climb a series of steep steps on the opposite side of the creek. The trail then heads through a group of huge, old buckeye trees, past a landslide, and to the site of an old Miwok village at Miwok Meadows.

Past the village site the trail heads out of the canyon and back into dense coast scrub. This side of the canyon is more moist, and the scrub is correspondingly greener.

The trail ends at Mesa Road, 0.75 mile from the trailhead. Turn left at the road and return to the parking lot at the field station.

The open ocean terraces of Point Reyes National Seashore offer plenty of solitude.

35. Coastal Trail to Bass Lake

Type:	Dayhike
Difficulty:	Difficult for children
Distance:	6 miles, round trip
Hiking time:	4 hours
Elevation gain:	400 feet
Hikable:	Year-round
Map:	Erickson's Map of Point Reyes National Seashore, Tomales Bay, and Taylor State Parks

This trail takes you into the Lakes District of Point Reyes National Seashore, which is very appropriate, since so much of the Point Reyes Peninsula has more than a passing resemblance to areas of the British Isles and is purported to include Sir Francis Drake's landing site during a layover in the early 1500s. Five lakes—Bass, Pelican, Crystal, Ocean, and Wildcat—are located along the Coastal Trail in the southern portion of Point Reyes National Seashore. They were created in part by movement of the nearby San Andreas Fault as earth slippage sealed off spring-fed creeks, thereby forming lakes. This area of the Point Reyes National Seashore is wild and rugged country with few visitors so wildlife is very

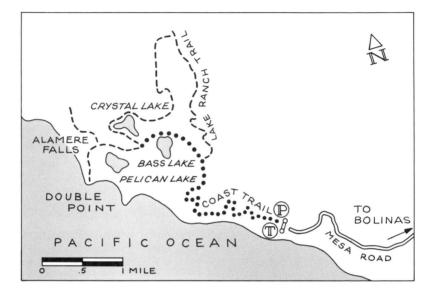

active. Bobcat and fox signs are often seen near the trail, and raccoon and deer tracks are as numerous as human tracks. Skunks and opossums are also found in large numbers around the berry patches.

Follow the directions for hike 34, Fern Canyon Trail, but continue on past the Point Reyes Bird Observatory Field Station for another mile to the end of the road. The trail leads out of the large parking lot located there.

After climbing into and through a stand of eucalyptus, the trail leads for about 1 mile along an open coastal shelf covered with coastal scrub interspersed with openings of grassland. Have the children smell the difference between the air in open grassland and that in the eucalyptus grove. They can pick up some freshly fallen leaves and crush them to discover that the pungent smell comes from the oil in the eucalyptus leaves. Wildflowers bloom profusely among the tall green grasses during early spring, and by June the grasses turn to a dull gray and summer weeds begin to bloom. Morning fog frequently hovers over the trail, obstructing views of the open ocean, but it generally burns away for clear afternoons.

At about 1 mile the trail goes around a large canyon, with thick riparian growth and cliffs reaching high above the trail. It descends into many ravines and canyons and climbs back to the terrace shelves. It repeats this several times, in and out of larger ravines, before turning inland through a small gorge full of ferns and live oaks. The Lake Ranch Trail junction is on the right just past the gorge. This is just over 2 miles from the trailhead and is less than 1 mile from Bass Lake.

Bass Lake is a 10-acre lake easily reached from the trail, and is a tranquil spot shaded by Douglas fir. This is a perfect spot to have a midday meal and rest stop before heading back to the trailhead. Waterfowl often land and feed here.

If you still feel like hiking, the trail leads on past Crystal and Pelican lakes and about 1 mile past Bass Lake a 0.5-mile side trail leads to Alamere Falls and Double Point. This last stretch is rather steep, but the views of the falls and the open ocean are spectacular during the spring after heavy winter rains. This extra hike makes the round trip about 8 miles.

36. Stewart/Greenpicker Trail Loop

Type: Dayhike
Difficulty: Difficult for children
Distance: 5.5 miles, loop
Hiking time: 4 hours
Elevation gain: 1100 feet
Hikable: Year-round
Map: Erickson's Map of
Point Reyes National
Seashore, Tomales Bay, and
Taylor State Parks

The 65,303 acres administered by the Point Reyes National Seashore comprise a wide variety of habitats and natural communities, and many of these can be reached by any of four different trailheads in the seashore. The first is Palomarin, which was the trailhead used in the previous two entries, hikes 34 and 35. This hike begins at the Five Brooks trailhead, and the trails that are accessible from here lead into rugged forested areas with plenty of wildlife. (Note that this hike may be too strenuous for children under 6 years of age.) The area is a geologically complex one as attested to by the fact that two parallel creeks in the area, Pine Gulch and Olema, drain in opposite directions.

Five Brooks trailhead is located off CA-1 about 3.5 miles south of Olema and 9 miles north of Stinson Beach. Turn west off CA-1 at the sign and drive about 0.25 mile up a gravel road past the horse stables to a large parking area. Stewart Trail, an old logging road, begins at the rear of the parking lot and circles a shallow duck pond that is covered with algae and encircled by tules and cattails.

The staff of Point Reyes uses Stewart Trail as an access route for vehicles to Wildcat Camp near the ocean, so it is kept in good condition. It cuts a wide, winding swath through a thick Douglas fir forest up toward the Ridge Trail and 1324-foot-high Firtop Meadow.

About 2 miles from the trailhead, a side trail leads off to the left from Stewart to Ridge Trail. Stay on Stewart and take a sharp right turn uphill and continue for 1 additional mile to Firtop Meadow. This large open meadow is an excellent place to stop for a picnic or rest before beginning the descent back to the trailhead.

Have your children explore the edge of the meadow in the transition zone where the low grass gives way to small bushes, that in turn give way to larger trees. See if they can find any evidence of whether the meadow is getting larger or is being encroached on by the forests. See if there is any sign of why animals might use the meadow: Do they use it for food, for shelter, or for both?

The junction of Stewart and Greenpicker Trails is about 0.25 mile past Firtop. Greenpicker is what appears to be an overgrown ranch road that is much narrower and steeper than Stewart for most of the way back to the trailhead. After about 0.5 mile of relatively open and level hiking from the junction with Stewart, Greenpicker begins a series of steep descents that drop 100 to 150 vertical feet within 75 to 100 yards. The

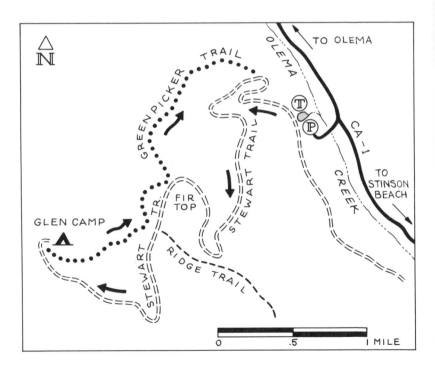

Ponds, such as this one at the Five Brooks trailhead, offer excellent birding opportunities.

first two drops have small, intimate meadows beside the trail where you can take a rest or explore. Steep descents sometimes cause hikers as much discomfort as steep climbs, and it is always wise to rest a short time after a particularly steep drop, especially for your younger hikers.

The rest of the trail is under the canopy of the fir forest, and is a continuing descent. Some seasonal creeks are located along the trail at spots, but generally only run for a short time after the rains stop.

A number of other hikes can be taken from the Five Brooks trailhead. Trail maps are available at the park visitor center at Bear Valley.

A hike in the back country of west Marin can be a lonely experience.

37. Peters Dam Hike

Type: Dayhike
Difficulty: Moderate for children
Distance: 1.5 miles, round trip
Hiking time: 1 hour
Elevation gain: 300 feet
Hikable: Year-round
Map: USGS Bolinas and
San Geronimo Topographic

Kent Lake is another of the many lakes administered by the Marin Municipal Water District in central and western Marin County, and it is much less used than the three lakes previously mentioned. The land around Kent is much wilder and the lake is long and slim and extends far up narrow canyons.

Take the Sir Francis Drake Boulevard exit off US 101 for about 14 miles to about 1 mile past the village of Lagunitas. At this point the road crosses Lagunitas (also known as Paper Mill) Creek. There is no parking near the green-railed fence, but about 300 yards farther down the road, past the sign for Samuel P. Taylor State Park, there is a small parking

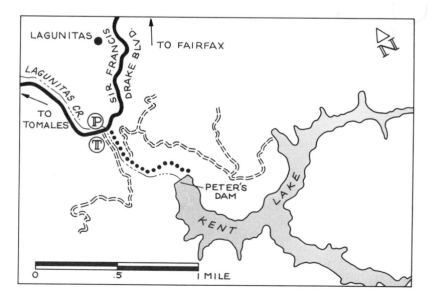

lot on the right side of the road. Park there and return to the bridge, where you turn right on the Marin Municipal Water District road, and head up Lagunitas Creek toward Peters Dam.

The walk to the dam is about 0.5 mile, and the last part is quite steep. The view from the dam is of wild, beautiful country where you can find solitude even on busy weekends. This is a good picnic and turnaround spot for families with young hikers. There are few trails in this rugged country, although a fire road leads off to the left about halfway to the dam and heads to one of the fingers of the lake. The forested slopes that lead down to the lake can be explored with relative ease from the dam area.

This short hike is more strenuous than most, and many families will be content to make the hike to the dam, have a picnic, explore the shoreline, and return to the parking area. This makes an excellent afternoon hike.

38. Wildcat Canyon Trail Loop

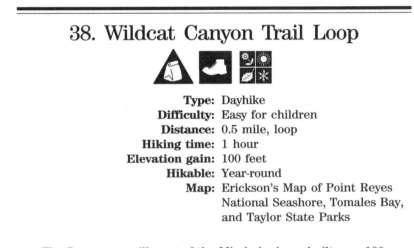

Type:	Dayhike
Difficulty:	Easy for children
Distance:	0.5 mile, loop
Hiking time:	1 hour
Elevation gain:	100 feet
Hikable:	Year-round
Map:	Erickson's Map of Point Reyes National Seashore, Tomales Bay, and Taylor State Parks

The first paper mill west of the Mississippi was built on a 100-acre site along Lagunitas Creek by Samuel Penfield Taylor in 1856. The site became a popular resort area for San Francisco residents, complete with hotel and campground, but all of it burned down in 1915. The property was bought by the Marin Conservation League in 1945 and turned over to the state for development as a park. Today it includes 2700 acres of second-growth redwoods and open hills. It is a popular hiking, bicycling, and horseback riding area.

Take the Sir Francis Drake Boulevard exit off US 101 and go about 16 miles west, passing the village of Lagunitas, to the signs for the park entrance. Park in the lot by the park office. You begin Wildcat Canyon

Cool picnics are the rule under the redwoods of Samuel P. Taylor State Park.

Trail at the Redwood Grove Picnic Area, which is across the creek from the main parking lot.

Wildcat Canyon Trail is a nature trail that loops through a redwood and Douglas fir forest. It is a good introduction to the various flora and fauna of the region, and it is an easy walk for the whole family. Be prepared to climb over or walk around fallen trees or branches, though, for the old trees in this grove often fall prey to the ravages of time and gravity. It takes a long time for redwood trees to decompose, and many of the fallen trees may have been on the ground for hundreds of years. Children like to pretend that they are early explorers wandering through the forests. Have them think about how the Native Americans of the region may have used the forests.

The trail crosses a small creek at about the halfway point, and on the way back down to the picnic area there is a magnificent pair of twin redwood trees on the left side of the trail.

The loop rejoins the original trail as it recrosses the small creek, and then returns to the picnic area.

39. Pioneer Tree Trail Loop

Type: Dayhike
Difficulty: Moderate for children
Distance: 2.5 miles, loop
Hiking time: 2 hours
Elevation gain: 200 feet
Hikable: Year-round
Map: Erickson's Map of Point Reyes National Seashore, Tomales Bay, and Taylor State Parks

The redwood trees that once covered the hillsides in the area were resistant to fire and disease, and one ancient tree still stands in the park as a tribute to the indestructible qualities of the species.

Follow the directions for hike 38, Wildcat Canyon Trail Loop, to the park. Pioneer Tree Trail begins at the Redwood Grove Picnic Area. Follow

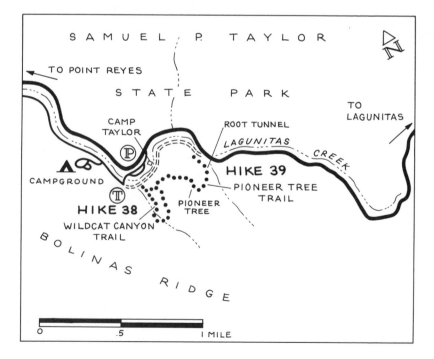

Large redwoods take centuries to decay.

the Old Railroad Grade Road from the picnic area; the Pioneer Tree Trail veers to the right just before the creek.

The trail leads over several small hills and then climbs slowly to the top of a small summit that offers views of Lagunitas Creek and the park. A bench is located here (about 0.75 mile from the trailhead) for those who like to sit on something substantial after a climb.

You head downhill for the next 0.25 mile, continue past a huge fallen fir tree, and soon come to the Pioneer Tree. This ancient redwood stands in the center of a circle of offspring trees that have sprouted from its roots, and has a deep fire scar that can hold several people at one time. The next tree also has a huge scar from the same fire. This spot is a good picnic area, with several benches for viewing the trees. Children love to play in the cavities formed by the fires.

The trail continues downhill for another 0.25 mile, and passes through a tunnel formed by giant tree roots before reaching the fire road that was the grade for the railroad that brought tourists to Camp Taylor and Point Reyes until about 1930. The road leads back to the picnic area along Lagunitas (Paper Mill) Creek.

Some bridges were built to withstand the ravages of time and weather.

40. Devil's Gulch Trail

Type: Dayhike
Difficulty: Difficult for children
Distance: 4 miles, round trip
Hiking time: 3 hours
Elevation gain: 200 feet
Hikable: Year-round
Map: Erickson's Map of Point Reyes National Seashore, Tomales Bay, and Taylor State Parks

Human habitation of the park region extends back hundreds of years, and the Devil's Gulch Trail follows part of an ancient Native American path that crossed Marin County. Devil's Gulch is on the opposite side of Sir Francis Drake Boulevard from the previous two entries, hikes 38 and 39. It is one of the most popular hikes in the park with its gentle climbs and deep forest setting.

 Follow the directions for hike 38, Wildcat Canyon Trail Loop, to Samuel P. Taylor State Park, but continue past the main park entrance for about 1 more mile to a parking lot on the right side of the road. The parking area is just past Devil's Gulch Creek.

The trail leads from the rear of the parking area and is between the creek and the fire road. Continue along the trail for about 0.5 mile to

116

a small clearing where there is a corral and picnic area. This is the approximate location of the dairy that served Taylorville in the late 1800s.

The clearing is about 0.5 mile long, and the trail then reenters the forest canopy that gives the gulch its special feel. The cool, moist environment is home to dozens of special plants that range from columbine and hound's tongue to orchids and nutmeg trees. These plants bloom from January to August and offer a continuous garden of delight.

At about 2 miles, the trail veers to the left to join the fire road and to the right to cross Devil's Gulch Creek. If you have hit it lucky, and there have been recent rains heavy enough to cause runoff to the creek to the left of the side trail, but not enough to keep you from rock-hopping across Devil's Gulch Creek, you can head up Stairstep Falls Trail. The climb of about 0.5 mile leads up some wooden steps. Have the kids count the number of steps. Then it runs along a gentle grade until Stairstep Falls appear crashing down about 40 feet over moss-covered rocks. This side trip adds about 1 mile to the hike, but is well worth the effort if the falls are full.

Return to the parking area along the creek. If you are hiking during late winter and early spring take this time to look for spawning salmon and steelhead trout. Children love to watch the fish make their tortuous swim upstream to reach their spawning grounds.

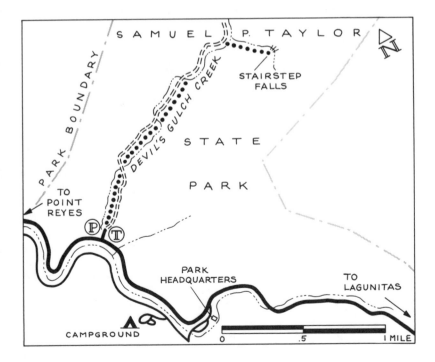

41. Barnabe Peak Trail Loop

Type: Dayhike
Difficulty: Difficult for children
Distance: 6 miles, loop
Hiking time: 4 hours
Elevation gain: 1300 feet
Hikable: Year-round
Map: Erickson's Map of Point Reyes
National Seashore, Tomales Bay,
and Taylor State Parks

The story has it that Barnabe was a mule that came to California with Colonel John C. Fremont in the 1840s and later became a pet for the Taylor children. The mountain reportedly became his favorite grazing area, and he learned to open all the gates that led up the trail. Supposedly, whenever he wandered off the family always knew where to find him. Today, while there are no mules on the mountain, the mountain is called Mount Barnabe, and serious hikers like to climb to the summit where they can enjoy the scenic views offered there.

Follow the directions for hike 38, Wildcat Canyon Trail Loop, to Samuel P. Taylor State Park. Park in the main parking lot by the park office. The trail to the summit begins at the Redwood Grove Picnic Area.

Take the Old Railroad Grade Road from the picnic area along Lagunitas Creek for about 0.75 mile to the footbridge that crosses the creek and leads across the road. This takes you to the Irving Picnic Area. Continue on the old road for another 0.5 mile to the junction with the Ridge Trail.

The grade to the top of 1466-foot Mount Barnabe begins as soon as you start up Ridge Trail, and continues to the peak. Along the creek, the trail leads through redwood, bay, and oak forest where shade-loving flowers can be seen most of the year, but it soon climbs above the forest into open grassland. Sun-loving wildflowers such as lupine and California poppies are often found in profuse bloom here.

The trail continues along the ridge for about 2 miles. The San Geronimo Valley can be seen to the east, and the village of Lagunitas can also be viewed. On a clear day, the top of Mount Tamalpais can be seen to the south, and Mount Diablo to the east.

As you approach the lookout tower operated by the Marin County Fire Department, glance back to catch a view of Kent Lake and Peters Dam. Although visitors are not allowed up in the fire lookout tower,

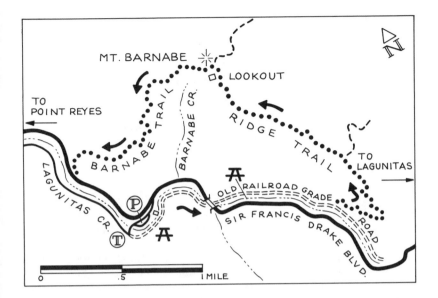

children can get a feel of how the fire fighters managing the lookout tower keep watch for forest fires all over western Marin County. Have them look out over a section of forest and envision a column of smoke rising from the trees. Then explain how two lookouts can calculate where the fire is by drawing lines on a map from each lookout toward the column of smoke, and where the two lines intersect on the map is where the fire is. Fire fighters can then quickly move to the site of the fire.

At the top of the peak, about 3.5 miles from the trailhead, the views to the north and west are stupendous. Point Reyes and Tomales Bay appear at your fingertips, and the Pacific Ocean is just beyond.

Return to the parking lot down the Barnabe Trail to the Madrone Group Area. This is about a 2.5-mile hike down the open mountain side. This stretch can be very warm and dry on a hot summer's day, but pleasant in the spring and fall.

42. Earthquake Trail

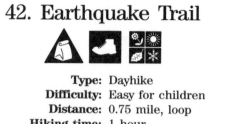

Type:	Dayhike
Difficulty:	Easy for children
Distance:	0.75 mile, loop
Hiking time:	1 hour
Elevation gain:	Minimal
Hikable:	Year-round
Map:	Erickson's Map of Point Reyes National Seashore, Tomales Bay, and Taylor State Parks

The Point Reyes Peninsula is really an island that sits on the western side of the San Andreas Fault. The peninsula has moved northward hundreds of miles from along the Southern California coast in the past several million years. Its position along the fault line makes it vulnerable to seismic activity, and it was, in fact, the epicenter of the great 1906

This fence is a graphic demonstration of earth movement during a major earthquake.

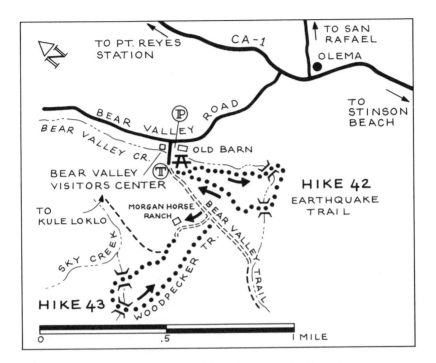

earthquake that destroyed San Francisco. There are still many visible examples of the movement along the fault at Point Reyes as a result of that quake, and Earthquake Trail near the Bear Valley Visitor Center of the Point Reyes National Seashore gives hikers an opportunity to see them.

Take CA-1 to Olema, and turn west on Bear Valley Road. The Bear Valley Visitor Center for Point Reyes National Seashore is just off Bear Valley Road, and Earthquake Trail lies to the east of the visitor center.

Earthquake Trail is a self-guided, 0.75-mile-long loop covered with asphalt. It begins at the restrooms at the picnic area across the road from the visitor center and crosses open grassland to reach the brambles near Bear Valley Creek. The trail turns to the left and follows along between the creek and a fence that was standing at the time of the 1906 quake. At about 0.5 mile there is information, with photos and an explanation of events, about how the fence was offset some 16 feet by the earth movement during the quake. Show your children the still-standing sections of fence that were offset by the quake to let them know how much 16 feet is.

The trail soon crosses back over Bear Valley Creek and heads back to the picnic area. This stretch of the trail passes by a number of large oak trees and through a wide variety of wildflowers that provide splotches of color to the green meadow from early spring to summer.

43. Woodpecker Trail

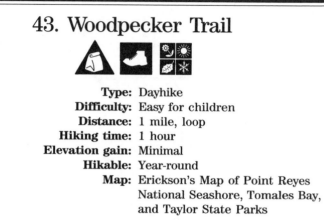

Type: Dayhike
Difficulty: Easy for children
Distance: 1 mile, loop
Hiking time: 1 hour
Elevation gain: Minimal
Hikable: Year-round
Map: Erickson's Map of Point Reyes National Seashore, Tomales Bay, and Taylor State Parks

Acorn woodpeckers are loud, raucous, and colorful residents of the Point Reyes National Seashore. They drill holes in large upright trees looking for insects, and later drive acorns into the holes for winter feasting. These "granary" trees become home to large family groups of the robin-sized birds with red heads, dark bodies, and white rumps.

Follow directions for hike 42, Earthquake Trail, to Bear Valley Visitor Center. The Woodpecker Trail begins at the Bear Valley Trail trailhead and heads uphill to the west. The first 0.25 mile of the trail leads you to the Morgan Horse Ranch barn and exhibits, and then veers off to the left just past the barn. The trail to the right continues around the corrals and to Kule Loklo, an authentic Native American village.

After veering to the left the trail leads through a fir forest that is alive with wildlife. Acorn woodpeckers, as well as numerous other birds, are very evident, especially during nesting time, and squirrels and deer are often seen. Two types of unusual deer live at Point Reyes, and they are frequently seen from this trail. One is the white fallow deer from Europe that was introduced into the area in the 1930s, and the other is the rare axis deer that was also introduced to the area. These two species are easily distinguished from the gray or brown deer that are native to the area. The fallow deer are all white and the axis deer have white spots on their backs even as adults. The axis deer generally live deep in forests, but they are relatively abundant at Point Reyes and are frequently seen. Keep an eye out for "granary" trees, generally large Douglas firs, which are dotted with the tips of hundreds of acorns stored by the acorn woodpeckers.

A footbridge crosses Sky Creek at a little less than 0.5 mile, and the trail continues through dense forest. It soon turns left, recrosses the creek, and emerges into a meadow that is covered with wildflowers in spring. From the meadow the trail returns to the Bear Valley Trail trailhead.

Acorn woodpeckers have been busy on this large fir tree.

44. Sky/Mount Wittenberg/Meadow Trail Loop

Type: Dayhike
Difficulty: Difficult for children
Distance: 6 miles, loop
Hiking time: 5 hours
Elevation gain: 1300 feet
Hikable: Year-round
Map: Erickson's Map of Point Reyes National Seashore, Tomales Bay, and Taylor State Parks

Sir Edmund Hillary is reported to have said that he climbed mountains because they were there, and it seems that most children were born with that feeling. Give a group of children a peak to climb and there frequently is no stopping them until they reach the top, especially if it is the highest point around. In Point Reyes that highest point is Mount Wittenberg at 1407 feet. Only a short distance from the Bear Valley Visitors Center as the crow flies, the hike to the summit is a steep, strenuous one that will challenge most youngsters and their families; it's not recommended for youngsters under 8 years of age.

Follow the directions for hike 42, Earthquake Trail, to the Bear Valley Visitors Center and head up the Bear Valley Trail. Sky Trail takes off to the right 0.2 mile past the Bear Valley trailhead.

Sky Trail is the nearest trail to the Bear Valley Visitors Center that leads to the top of Mount Wittenberg, but it is also the steepest. It climbs about 1300 feet in less than 2 miles from the Bear Valley Trail. This is not an uninterrupted torture, however, for there are many tree-shaded segments of the trail, and the open areas often have a wide variety of wildflowers to observe during rests. There are also patches of coastal scrub along the trail that are home to many small birds.

Although parts of the trail pass through dense forest, you will notice the lack of redwoods that would be on most other trails in western Marin County. Although most of the other trees that generally accompany redwoods (bay, tanoak, and Douglas fir) are found along the trail, redwoods cannot grow on the granitic soil of Point Reyes.

At 1.6 miles from the Bear Valley trailhead, Sky Trail is joined by the Mount Wittenberg Trail on the right. Follow this trail for less than 0.5 mile to its highest point. This point is to the west of the peak, and you have to bushwhack up the hillside for several hundred yards to reach the top. This is somewhat anticlimactic, though, for the dense tree cover on the peak blocks out any vistas that might be visible. The views from the Mount Wittenberg and Sky trails are much better.

Continue on past the peak for about 0.2 mile, where the trail dead ends, and turn right on the Horse Trail. Go for about 0.4 mile to the junction of Horse, Sky, and Fire Lane trails. Turn left on Sky Trail. For the next mile there are splendid views of Drakes Estero, Point Reyes, and the Pacific Ocean as you walk along an open section of old fire road.

Bishop pines, an unusual tree for this region of northern California, are found in several groves along this section of trail. Have the children try to identify this 50- to 75-foot-tall pine with its unusual flat or very rounded top and generally grotesque shape. The Bishop pine also has hard, tight cones with sharp prickles on the ends of each scale. The seeds in these cones only germinate after they have been exposed to a fire. Therefore, the Bishop pine and several others whose seeds only germinate after a fire are known as "fire" pines. Have the children discuss what survival benefits this would give to the trees. (Since the young trees of these species need plenty of sunlight to grow, they have a distinct advantage if they germinate after a fire has destroyed the canopy of the forest. This canopy would have provided too much shade for seedlings before the fire.)

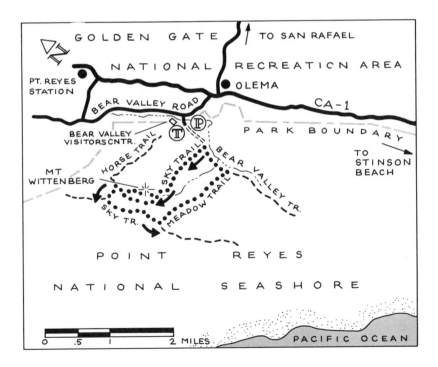

A miniature meadow sits at the junction of Sky Trail and Meadow Trail, and is an excellent place to stop and rest before you begin the 1.5-mile, 1000-foot descent to the Bear Valley Trail.

Meadow Trail begins its sharp descent through huckleberry bushes, and an occasional toyon or alder before reentering the fir forest. At about 1 mile from the junction with Sky Trail (4.7 miles from the trailhead), Meadow Trail leaves the forest and enters a steep, sunlit meadow that is generally green year-round. This meadow is about 200 yards across and is a good stopping point. On cool days you can rest in the sunlight; on warm days you can rest on the edge of the forest.

The closeup world of small animals and plants that can be found in the turf of the meadow is fascinating to children. Have them use a hand lens to look at the small flowers, seeds, and insects found in the weeds and grasses in the meadow.

The trail descends another 400 feet in the next 0.5 mile before it turns left onto the Bear Valley Trail. From there it is 0.8 mile to the trailhead.

45. Bear Valley Trail

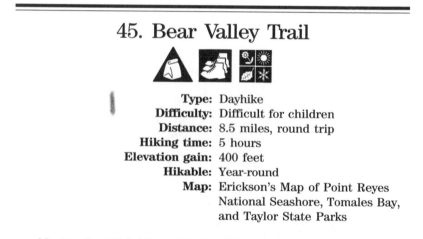

Type: Dayhike
Difficulty: Difficult for children
Distance: 8.5 miles, round trip
Hiking time: 5 hours
Elevation gain: 400 feet
Hikable: Year-round
Map: Erickson's Map of Point Reyes National Seashore, Tomales Bay, and Taylor State Parks

Most trails at Point Reyes National Seashore require a considerable amount of climbing, but the Bear Valley Trail that begins near the rear of the Bear Valley Visitors Center gains and loses less than 400 feet over its 4+ miles. This makes it one of the most popular trails in the seashore. The trek along Bear Valley Creek to Arch Rock on the coast is pleasant and leads through open grassland, forests of Bishop pine and douglas fir, and stretches of coastal scrub. Bear Valley Trail follows the route of an old wagon trail (a hunting lodge that hosted such luminaries as Presidents William Howard Taft and Theodore Roosevelt once stood at Divide Meadows), and is wide enough for several people to walk abreast. Deer, bear, mountain lions, and game birds were abundant during the early part of this century, but few of these other than deer are seen today.

Follow directions for hike 42, Earthquake Trail, to Bear Valley Visitors Center and the trailhead for Bear Valley Trail.

The first 0.25 mile of the trail is open and fairly populated with hikers, but it enters a forest of tall pine and fir trees just past the junction with the Sky Trail. Hikers soon begin to thin out, but many continue on for 1.5 miles to Divide Meadows, a green meadow surrounded by dense forest where there are picnic tables and chemical toilets.

Divide Meadows was aptly named because it is the spot where Bear Valley Creek, which runs north to Tomales Bay, is separated from Coast Creek, which runs south to the ocean. This drainage pattern is the result of land movement along the San Andreas Fault.

During late spring and summer, berries of many types are found along the sides of the creek. Blackberries, thimbleberries, huckleberries, salal berries, and elderberries all provide food and shelter to many small birds, and offer delicious snacks for hikers. While almost all of the berries along this stretch of trail are safe to eat, you should check with the rangers at the visitor center about which ones are safe if you are not sure of your ability to identify the berries. While they are in abundance during certain times of the year, they aren't so plentiful that they can

be collected in large containers. Pick some for a refreshing snack and to give your children a chance to taste some wild berries, but leave most for other hikers and the many animals and birds that live in the area.

For almost the entire distance from Sky Trail to the ocean, Bear Valley Trail has a canopy of alders, laurels, fir, and bay that makes it a delightful walk on hot summer days. It can be somewhat drippy after a winter rain or during foggy times. One of these old bay trees alongside the creek, located about 2.5 miles from the trailhead, offers a delightful rest stop where youngsters can climb and explore.

The trail continues on a slight descent from Divide Meadows to the ocean, and several longer trails lead off it to both the north and south in the last 2 miles.

Bear Valley Trail ends with a short climb down a path to a beach and Arch Rock. At low tide adventurous hikers can crawl beneath the arch, but care should be taken that waves aren't breaking over the rock.

Children like to explore along the trail down to the beach, and along the beach after the long hike from the visitor center. Have them watch the waves break over the rocks along the shore, and then see if they can explain how Arch Rock was formed.

Return to the visitor center along the same route.

Even the crowded trails of Point Reyes National Seashore can be quiet.

46. Muddy Hollow/Estero Trail

Type: Dayhike
Difficulty: Difficult for children
Distance: 6 miles, round trip
Hiking time: 3 hours
Elevation gain: 200 feet
Hikable: Year-round
Map: Erickson's Map of Point Reyes National Seashore, Tomales Bay, and Taylor State Parks

The region around Drakes Estero in the northwest section of Point Reyes has no broad beaches, dense forests, high hills, or other scenic vistas. It is open rolling country with abundant wildlife, spring and summer wildflowers, and its often fog-shrouded views are more reminiscent of Scotland's moors than of California's golden hills. It is attractive to hikers, though, because the wildlife is very visible, the wildflowers colorful, and the hiking is easy. Bobcat, axis deer, fallow deer, marsh hawks, pelicans, geese, herons, and egrets are only a few of the animals you will see as you hike the rolling terrain. Coyote bush, lupine, monkeyflower, and elderberry are some of the plants that cover the hillsides.

Take Bear Valley Road west from Olema, and turn left on Limantour Road about 1 mile past the visitor center. At about 7 miles (at the signs for the American Youth Hostel and the Clem Miller Education Center) make a right turn and continue for a short distance to the parking lot. Take the Muddy Hollow Trail southwest toward the ocean.

The first 1.4 miles of the trail follow along a creek through a seepy area that gives the trail its name. The creek banks are covered with willow and alder, and berries form thick brambles. Just past 1 mile there is a small, freshwater pond on the right of the trail where waterfowl often feed and nest. The saltwater of Estero de Limantour is kept out of the pond and creek by an earthen dam.

There are many differences in the plants and animals that live and feed in freshwater and those that do so in saltwater. Have your children look for some of the differences in the plants and animals in the freshwater pond and those in Limantour Estero, which is saltwater.

At 1.25 miles, Muddy Hollow Trail veers to the left and Estero Trail joins it to the right. Take Estero up a small hill. The landscape changes dramatically here as coastal scrub covers the hillsides. About 1 mile from Muddy Hollow Trail, Estero Trail crosses Glenbrook Creek by a wooden

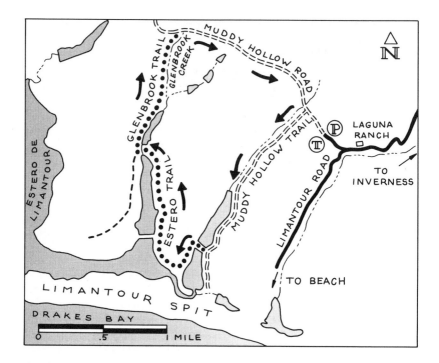

footbridge and heads up a long, gentle climb. A grove of eucalyptus trees offers a shady spot for a picnic just past the bridge. The trail continues upward past the grove, and soon passes an old dam that was washed out in heavy rains in 1982.

From the junction of Estero and Muddy Hollow trails to Estero and Glenbrook Trails there are excellent views of Drakes Bay, Point Reyes Head, and the white cliffs that are reminiscent of the cliffs of Dover.

Two miles from Muddy Hollow Trail, Estero Trail joins Glenbrook Trail. Take Glenbrook to the right as Estero turns sharply to the left, and continue on it for 0.7 mile to Muddy Hollow Road. Turn right and return for 1.4 miles to the trailhead.

47. Limantour Spit Trail

Type: Dayhike
Difficulty: Easy for children
Distance: 2 to 4 miles, round trip
Hiking time: 3 hours
Elevation gain: None
Hikable: Year-round
Map: Erickson's Map of Point Reyes
National Seashore, Tomales Bay,
and Taylor State Parks

Limantour Spit is one of the longest sandbars on the west coast, and separates Estero de Limantour from Drakes Bay. Drakes Estero joins with Estero de Limantour at the end of Limantour Spit. Sand spits such as Limantour are formed by littoral currents that parallel the shore and

The salt marshes at Limantour Beach teem with life.

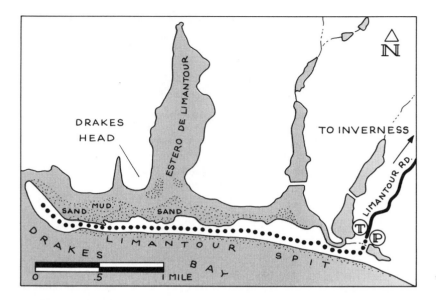

deposit sand at the mouth of esteros, where water is too calm to keep sand suspended. Limantour is about 2 miles long, and has been set aside as a natural area.

 Follow the directions for hike 46, Muddy Hollow/Estero Trail, but continue on Limantour Road to the parking lot at the end. A paved path leads through ponds and marshes from the parking lot to the beach.

This hike is more free-form than most of the others in this guide because there are numerous small trails that lead off the beach into the marshlands on the estero side, and the beach is open for either long or short walks.

Hikers who take some of the side trails, and/or walk all the way to the end of the spit, may hike as much as 4 miles round trip, while those who stay pretty much to the center of the spit, and only go about halfway to the end, will only hike about 2 miles round trip.

Harbor seals, shorebirds, and waterfowl are all found here in abundance, and a walk along the beach or into the marshlands is a birdwatcher's dream. Even raccoon prints can frequently be spotted near the end of the spit where grassy mounds become islands during high tide.

During weekends in the full bloom of spring the beach is crowded, but more stimulating hikes can be found during the beginning or end of winter storms when the beach becomes a wild, windswept refuge from civilization, and hikers have little company. Children enjoy hiking along the spit after heavy winter storms because vast quantities of drift material are to be found along the beach. They like to fantasize about where the material came from and what caused it to be in the ocean.

48. Tomales Bay Trail

Type: Dayhike
Difficulty: Moderate for children
Distance: 2.5 miles, round trip
Hiking time: 2 hours
Elevation gain: Minimal
Hikable: Year-round
Map: Erickson's Map of Point Reyes
National Seashore, Tomales Bay,
and Taylor State Parks

The 12-mile-long Tomales Bay is a submerged rift of the San Andreas Fault. The steep, wooded slopes of the Point Reyes Peninsula are typical of the Pacific Plate, and the gently rolling hills covered with grass are typical of the North American Plate. In earlier times, Tomales Bay extended southward to connect with Bolinas Lagoon, but a temporary landfill has connected Point Reyes with the mainland. This fill is marshlands that are home to hundreds of small animals and birds and are feeding grounds for a wide variety of shore birds and waterfowl. In 1990 the 260-acre Elmer Martinelli Ranch was purchased and made part of the Golden Gate

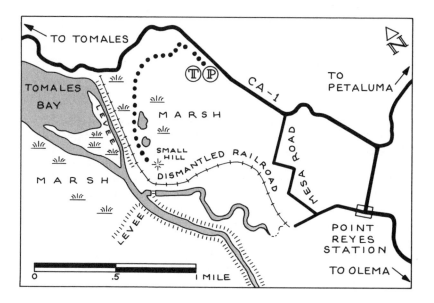

An old pasture makes for easy walking near Tomales Bay.

National Recreation Area, and a 1.3-mile-long trail has been developed that crosses the ranch land from CA-1 to the bay shore.

Take CA-1 north of Point Reyes Station. A small parking lot is located on the west side of the highway almost exactly 1 mile north of the Bank of America building in Point Reyes Station. A narrow footpath is marked with a National Park Service sign and leads out from the north end of the parking lot.

The trail heads down a small draw toward a large, poison-oak-covered boulder and some boards that cross a wet stretch of the trail. From there it veers to the left and heads uphill. At the top of the ridge you have a wide-angle vista of Tomales Bay and the village of Inverness on the opposite side of the bay.

At just less than 0.5 mile, the trail crosses an old ranch road. Follow the trail markers to the left and head downhill. Two small ponds encircled by cattails and rushes that are home to redwing blackbirds, cormorants, herons, and egrets are on the left. This is an excellent spot for kids to explore and hunt for small animals such as frogs and tadpoles.

Just past the second pond, you cross a small weir and climb uphill to reach a knoll that overlooks Tomales Bay. Ahead is a large marsh area that is active with birds and small mammals that feed the rich marshlands.

Several long levees that cross the marsh are the remains of 12 miles of fill and trestles that carried the North Pacific Coast Railroad across the low-lying area in the early 1900s.

49. Heart's Desire/Indian Beach Trail Loop

Type: Dayhike
Difficulty: Easy for children
Distance: 1 mile, loop
Hiking time: 2 hours
Elevation gain: Minimal
Hikable: Year-round
Map: Erickson's Map of Point Reyes National Seashore, Tomales Bay, and Taylor State Parks

The beaches of Tomales Bay State Park are located on the east side of Inverness Ridge, and they are sheltered from much of the wind and fog that are common on the beaches of Point Reyes National Seashore a few miles away on the west side of the ridge. The waters off the beaches

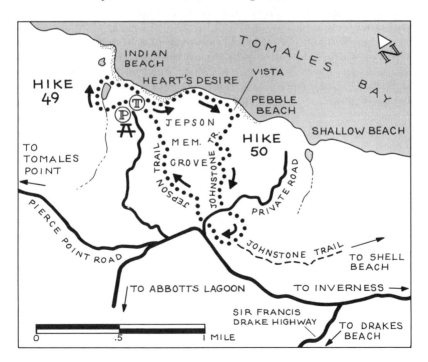

here are also surf-free and shallow, although not much warmer than those on the Pacific. There are four popular beaches in the park, but this hike covers only the two closest to the parking lot. Clamming for horseneck, littleneck, Washington, and gaper clams is allowed on all the beaches for those who have a valid California fishing license. (Children under the age of 16 do not need a fishing license, but any adults who help them clam must have one.)

 Take Sir Francis Drake Highway west from CA-1 just south of Point Reyes Station for 2.5 miles to Pierce Point Road. Turn right and follow the signs to Tomales Bay State Park. Enter the park and continue to the parking area near Heart's Desire Beach and the picnic area.

Heart's Desire is the most accessible and most popular beach in the park, but you quickly lose much of the crowd as you begin the 0.5-mile nature trail between Heart's Desire and Indian Beaches. This well-marked trail includes sign posts that tell how the Miwok Indians used many of the native plants of the area such as toyon and coffee berries and the fruit of the bay trees. The trail climbs slightly for about 0.25 mile before dropping down onto Indian Beach. This beach is a sandy point that juts out into the bay, and it has water and restrooms. This is a good place to have a picnic, but your children may want to hike around the marsh that lies just inland from the beach. They can see shorebirds and waterfowl feeding here, and see and hear many small animals if they sit quietly near the edge of the marsh. Great blue herons and snowy egrets also often feed here.

Listen and you may hear the eerie call of a loon here during the summer, when flights of brown pelicans may also be seen offshore.

After you have taken the loop trail around the marsh you can rest at Indian Beach before taking the short nature walk back to Heart's Desire Beach.

50. Johnstone/Jepson Trail Loop

Type: Dayhike
Difficulty: Moderate for children
Distance: 3 miles, loop
Hiking time: 2 hours
Elevation gain: 300 feet
Hikable: Year-round
Map: Erickson's Map of Point Reyes National Seashore, Tomales Bay, and Taylor State Parks

While the beaches are the most popular area of Tomales Bay State Park there are plenty of other interesting sights in the over 1000 acres in the park. The ridge just inland from the beaches is covered with a thick forest of Bishop pine, madrone, bay, various oaks, and buckeye. An occasional chinquapin is also seen. The Bishop pine grove on the ridge is one of the finest virgin groves left in California. These pine are grotesquely shaped relatives of the Monterey pine, and belong to a group of "closed-cone pines" that have survived from prehistoric forests. The tightly closed, prickly cones do not open to disperse their seeds as most pine cones, but must first be exposed to fire or extreme heat before opening. This means that the seeds are rarely dispersed.

Follow the directions to Tomales Bay State Park given in hike 49, Heart's Desire/Indian Beach Trail Loop. The Johnstone Trail begins at the south end of Heart's Desire Beach.

The trail climbs almost immediately into a dense, moss-draped forest of oak, bay, and madrone. There is a picnic and vista area at 0.5 mile on a bluff above Pebble Beach. Just past this a short trail leads off to Pebble Beach, but Johnstone Trail swings inland and begins a series of switchbacks up the slope toward the ridge. Many varieties of fern are found along this protected section of the trail.

This section of the trail also has many varieties of moss and lichen. Have the children observe the differences among these primitive plants and see how many different types they can find along the trail.

The trail crosses a paved road at about 1 mile, and soon comes to a junction. Johnstone Trail continues to the left for 3 miles to Shell Beach. Jepson Trail heads straight and leads back to Heart's Desire Beach.

This section of Jepson Trail leads through Jepson Memorial Grove, a virgin grove of Bishop pine, a slowly propagating fire pine that is rare along California's north coast (the closest stand comparable to the Jepson

Grove is located in Montana de Oro State Park in San Luis Obispo County).

The trail from the grove back to Heart's Desire Beach is a slow descent with several excellent vista stops where benches have been located to give hikers an opportunity to enjoy the views overlooking Tomales Bay.

The trees at Tomales Bay State park are frequently covered with beards of lichen.

51. Tomales Point Trail

Type: Dayhike
Difficulty: Difficult for children
Distance: 6 to 9 miles, round trip
Hiking time: 4 to 5 hours
Elevation gain: 300 feet
Hikable: Year-round
Map: Erickson's Map of Point Reyes
National Seashore, Tomales Bay,
and Taylor State Parks

Just past Tomales Bay State Park, Tomales Point and Upper Pierce Ranch, a fog-shrouded grassland that was once home to a flourishing dairy, jut out as the northernmost boundary of Marin County and the Point Reyes National Seashore. This exposed spit of land can be extremely windy and is often colder than any other area in the seashore, but this only adds to the feeling of solitude that you'll get along this stretch of coastal plains. On this hike you are more likely to encounter tule elk than people because this is a designated tule elk range. Other than elk, the wildlife you will see will probably be limited to small birds flitting in the coastal scrub and raptors soaring overhead. Vegetation is also sparse along the trail with grass, bush lupine, some coastal scrub, and little else.

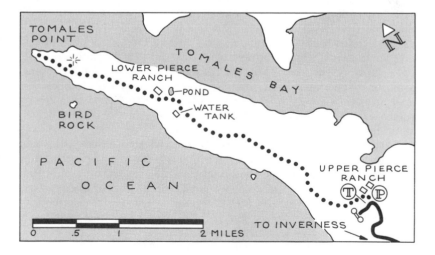

You are as likely to see a tule elk as another person on the trail to Tomales Point.

Follow the directions to Tomales Bay State Park given in hike 49, Heart's Desire/Indian Beach Trail Loop, but continue on past the park entrance on Pierce Point Road (follow signs for McClures Beach). The parking area is 9 miles from the junction of Sir Francis Drake Highway and Pierce Point Road. Park at the ranch, which is about 0.25 mile before the parking lot for McClures Beach. Follow the old dirt road around the ranch to the west to get on the trail to Tomales Point.

The first mile of the trail, which is an old ranch road that provides a wide, level walking surface, closely follows the contours of the cliffs on the ocean side of the point. It makes a gradual ascent of a small ridge as it turns in from the ocean, and as you reach the crest you have views of both the ocean and 15-mile-long Tomales Bay, with good views of Hog Island and Dillon's Beach. There are small outcroppings of granite all along the trail, which is unusual for this region of California.

At 3 miles from the trailhead you come to the second unit of the old Pierce Ranch, which operated from 1869 until 1980. There is a pond and a grove of eucalyptus trees at the sight, which is a good stopping point for lunch and a turnaround. For those that still want to hike, the 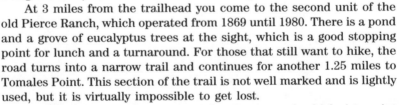 road turns into a narrow trail and continues for another 1.25 miles to Tomales Point. This section of the trail is not well marked and is lightly used, but it is virtually impossible to get lost.

About 1 mile past the second ranch unit, you reach a high vista point that overlooks Bird Rock to the west, which is home to many cormorants and white pelicans. You can continue for another several hundred yards to the very top of Tomales Point for outstanding views of Bodega Bay, Dillon's Beach, and Tomales Bay. The point is a series of granite cliffs and outcroppings, something that is found only to the west of the San Andreas Fault in this section of the coast.

Return to the trailhead along the same route.

52. Abbott's Lagoon Trail

Type:	Dayhike
Difficulty:	Moderate for children
Distance:	3 miles, round trip
Hiking time:	2 hours
Elevation gain:	200 feet
Hikable:	Year-round
Map:	Erickson's Map of Point Reyes National Seashore, Tomales Bay, and Taylor State Parks

There is something haunting and lonely about the land on the ocean side of Point Reyes Peninsula, and the land around Abbott's Lagoon certainly fits that description. The hills are covered with grass that is green during late winter and spring, but a dull gray the rest of the year, salt-tanged winds sweep in off the ocean, fog often hangs overhead all day, and only yellow and blue bush lupines add noticeable splotches of color to an otherwise monochrome vista. Even the water of the lagoon (actually a pair of lagoons separated by a narrow isthmus of land) takes on a gray hue on most days. With that said, this can be an invigorating hike. The air is always brisk, there are seldom any other hikers to break

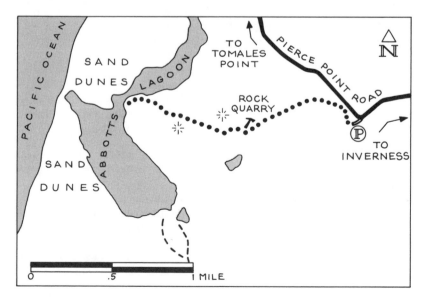

the solitude of the moors, and the beach is always a spot to watch shore-birds flit and feed.

Follow the directions to Tomales Bay State Park given in hike 49, Heart's Desire/Indian Beach Trail Loop, and continue past the park entrance on Pierce Point Road for 1.5 miles to a small parking lot with toilets on the west side of the road. The trail to the lagoon leads out of the parking lot.

The hike is simple, the trail is gentle, and the view is unobstructed as you wind your way down the trail from the road to the upper reaches of the lagoon. Shorebirds and waterfowl, as well as occasional small animals, can always be viewed near the lagoon, and the sand dunes before the beach offer good seats for adults for contemplation and viewing while the kids run, jump, and slide on the sides of the dunes. This fun activity is an excellent way for them to work off some energy as the adults view the ocean.

A small stream drains the lagoons into a small pool at the beach, from which the water gently makes its way to the ocean. This is a good spot to take a rest or eat lunch before heading back to the parking area.

---

53. Estero Trail

Type: Dayhike
Difficulty: Difficult for children
Distance: 8 miles, round trip
Hiking time: 5 hours
Elevation gain: 300 feet
Hikable: Year-round
Map: Erickson's Map of Point Reyes National Seashore, Tomales Bay, and Taylor State Parks

Drakes Estero is home to harbor seals, leopard sharks, stingrays, and is an important resting spot for thousands of waterfowl. It is also a food source for many species of shorebirds. With all of this wildlife, you will want to bring your binoculars on this hike. During the spring and early summer the hills are emblazoned with wildflowers, and the days are generally sunny until the summer pattern of morning fog begins. The estero is a drowned valley that was flooded by the rising ocean after the last ice age, and it was once deep enough for large vessels to anchor in. Natural erosion patterns have since filled in the estero so that now it is non-navigable.

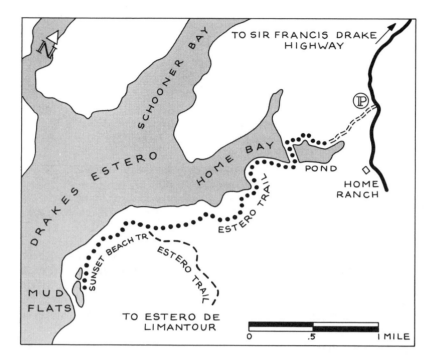

Take Sir Francis Drake Highway off CA-1, and continue past the road to Mount Vision. Less than 1 mile later you will see a road sign for the Estero Trail parking lot.

This hike only takes you on the first part of the Estero Trail as it leads you alongside Drakes Estero for most of the way. From the parking lot you follow an old ranch road on a gentle climb. As you look back over your shoulder you can see Mount Vision, Point Reyes Hill, and Mount Wittenberg along Inverness Ridge. The trail turns to the left and passes a small stand of pine. Have the kids guess what these pines were used for. (They're part of what was once a Christmas-tree farm.)

At about 1 mile the trail crosses a causeway that divides Home Bay from a small pond. Large numbers of shorebirds feed in the mudflats of Home Bay. The trail climbs above the bay for a short distance, and then drops down to another small pond, after which it climbs again.

At about 2.5 miles there is a junction; Estero Trail turns left and Sunset Beach Trail continues straight. If your little ones are getting tired this is a good spot to rest and then begin a hike back to the parking lot. Otherwise continue on Sunset Beach Trail for another 1.5 miles as it climbs well above the estero. It ends at a couple of small freshwater ponds where you can picnic with views of Drakes Bay and the Pacific.

Return by the same route.

54. Drakes Beach Trail

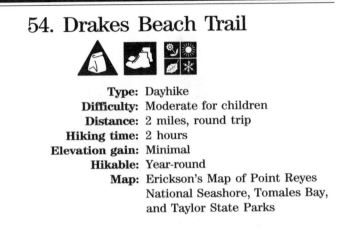

Type: Dayhike
Difficulty: Moderate for children
Distance: 2 miles, round trip
Hiking time: 2 hours
Elevation gain: Minimal
Hikable: Year-round
Map: Erickson's Map of Point Reyes National Seashore, Tomales Bay, and Taylor State Parks

Drakes Beach is the site of historical controversy and an outdoor lover's delight. Many historians think that this beach is where Sir Francis Drake and his crew on the *Golden Hind* laid over for some months while they were exploring the West Coast in the sixteenth century. Others think they actually entered San Francisco Bay and laid over somewhere near Tiburon.

The long open beach, white cliffs, and sweeping vistas are enough without any other offerings, but many people come to Drakes Bay to hike

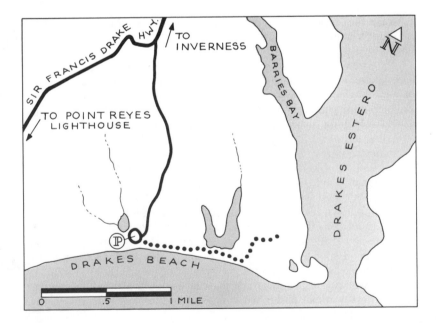

The whole family can enjoy the beach at Drakes Bay.

along the beach and to the edge of Drakes Estero, where birdwatching
is unmatched.

Take Sir Francis Drake Highway off CA-1 just south of Point Reyes
Station, and continue on it for 14 miles to the parking lot for Drakes
Beach.

Hike down the beach away from the crowded parking lot area. At
about 0.5 mile, a trail heads inland off to the left. This loops to the east
of a small lagoon that is home to many shorebirds, and heads uphill to
overlook much larger Drakes Estero, one of the prime birding spots on
the Point Reyes Peninsula. The loop is about 1 mile, and the overlook
of the estero is an excellent place to have a snack or picnic.

Return to the beach and head back toward the parking lot. Travel
slowly along the water's edge and you may find small shells, crabs, and
jellyfish. Have the children count how many types of shells they can find
along the beach, as well as look for small jellyfish that have washed
ashore and become covered with sand. Don't collect these beach trea-
sures, but look them over well.

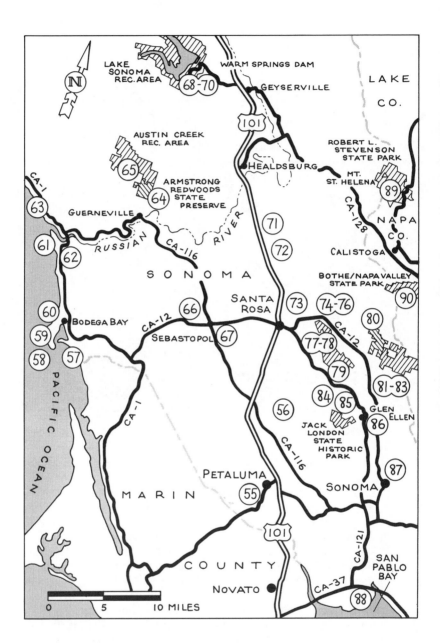

Sonoma County

Nature constantly tries to reclaim space from human use.

55. Trail Loop

Type: Dayhike
Difficulty: Moderate for children
Distance: 2 miles, loop
Hiking time: 2 hours
Elevation gain: 400 feet
Hikable: Year-round
Map: USGS Petaluma Topographic

Sonoma County has made a concerted effort to develop a series of regional parks that help preserve at least small segments of the natural environment in the area as urbanization has encroached on what was until recently a rural, agricultural county. Helen Putnam County Park is one of those parks, and it is located just north of the Marin/Sonoma County line outside Petaluma. The land in the park is typical of southern Sonoma County—rolling to steep grass-covered hills with oak woodlands—and offers a number of walks within its 200+ acres. Views are excellent on clear days, and wildflowers cover the hillsides during the spring.

Take the Washington Street exit off US 101 in Petaluma. Continue west toward the center of town and turn left on Petaluma Boulevard. Take the first right, Western Avenue, and go about 2 miles to Chileno Valley Road. Turn left on Chileno Valley and go for just less than 1 mile to the park entrance.

The trail begins about 150 feet along the paved service road from the parking area near the restrooms, where there is a large map of the park. Head left on the trail from the map and turn right at the first redwood post marked with an arrow. The first half of the trail is marked with these posts.

The trail descends gently just past the first marker, and you duck under the limb of an old oak as you begin to climb out of the gully. From here you climb into open grassland dotted with oaks. The trail levels out at about 0.25 mile and overlooks an old ranch that is outside the park boundaries. Soon afterward the trail merges with a broader one, goes through a gate, and comes to a small pond. This is a good place to stop and explore. Your children can look for frogs and small fish among the cattails and tules that grow along the shore of the pond. They can also see how many types of dragonflies they can find among the plants. There should be blue, green, and black ones.

As you leave the pond, cross the dam and turn left on the paved path that follows the shore of the pond. Along this section of the trail wildflowers such as daffodils, poppies, and lupine cover the open land between the pond and the trail during the spring and early summer.

Past the pond, angle right on the path where oaks grow along the park boundary. Continue uphill until you pass through a fence and come to a multitude of trails. One on the left is marked with a redwood post. Take that one and climb for about 200 feet. Take a lightly traveled trail off to the right, where it comes close to the paved path before turning left to follow the line of oaks. It soon enters the oak forest and follows the contour of the hillside.

The scenery along this section ranges from the subdivisions of Petaluma to views of Mount St. Helena and Sonoma Mountain.

A large California buckeye stands alongside the trail, and various wildflowers such as mariposa lily and brodiaea can be seen during the spring. Unfortunately, poison oak grows in profusion along several sections of the trail also.

Just before 1 mile the trail dips and then climbs to offer fantastic views to the north. Mount St. Helena, Sonoma Mountain, and Bennett Mountain all stand out on clear days as the steam plumes from the geysers remind you of the volcanic origin of all the peaks. A small open meadow surrounded by oaks is often the sight of feeding deer in early morning and evening.

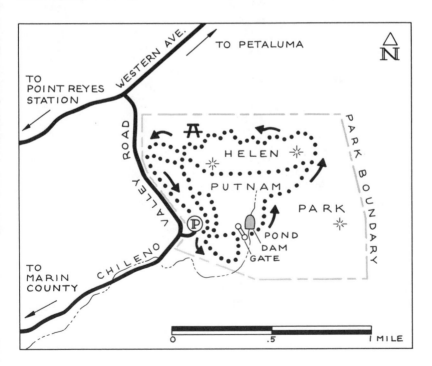

At 1 mile there is a short, steep climb to the ridge, and there you will find picnic tables with views of Sonoma and Marin County hills.

The trail turns south after the picnic tables, and comes to a junction of several trails after another 200 yards. Take the far right trail, which leads to the ridge after a short climb. There you are at the park boundary. The trail begins to descend to the left and then it forks. The right fork would take you along the steep boundary trail back to the parking area; instead take the left fork, which leads you along a more gentle hike. It descends, crosses a broad path, and then climbs uphill again, all in about 200 yards. It then meets another, well-traveled path. Turn right on this trail and climb for a short distance to the ridge. The trail splits again

Looking for small animals makes for a pleasant break on the trail.

as you begin your descent. Take the left fork that gradually descends into a small oak-filled canyon. At the next trail junction turn right and head down the canyon to the south.

From there the trail crosses open grasslands to the trailhead.

56. Native Plant Trail

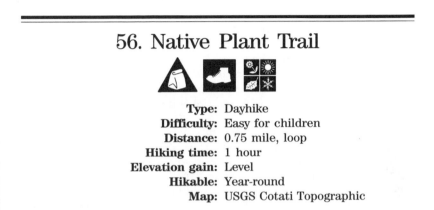

Type: Dayhike
Difficulty: Easy for children
Distance: 0.75 mile, loop
Hiking time: 1 hour
Elevation gain: Level
Hikable: Year-round
Map: USGS Cotati Topographic

Many colleges and universities have arboretums and native plant gardens, and Sonoma State University in Rohnert Park/Cotati is no exception. This short trail includes plants from a number of habitats, and finishes with a long stretch along a creek bank, where native willows and alders represent the dominant plants of this riparian habitat. The trail is lightly used during weekends and vacation periods because most students are away from campus and few local residents use the trail.

Take the Rohnert Park Expressway exit off US 101 in Rohnert Park and head east. Continue for about 2.5 miles to the end of the expressway at Petaluma Hill Road. Turn right on Petaluma Hill Road for less than 0.5 mile to Sonoma State University. Take a right on the first street into the campus, go past the tennis courts, and park in the first available lot. On weekends and holidays parking is free, but there is a fee for days when school is in session. The native plant trail is located just north of the gym.

The trail begins with examples of plants that prefer dry exposed areas, and winds through exhibits of a variety of plants for about 0.25 mile. As the trail turns toward Copeland Creek examples appear of larger trees and shrubs native to the region. At a little less than 0.5 mile, the trail takes a sharp turn to the left, leads down to the creek, and begins a loop back to the beginning.

The last 0.25 mile or so goes through the tangle of riparian growth found near the creek, and offers a good place to explore creek life during late spring after the flow of winter runoff has slowed, but before the creek has dried up for the summer and fall.

57. Pinnacle Gulch Trail

Type: Dayhike
Difficulty: Moderate for children
Distance: 1 mile, round trip
Hiking time: 1 hour
Elevation gain: 200 feet
Hikable: Year-round
Map: USGS Bodega Head Topographic

Although Sonoma County is second from last among California counties in the amount of land in public ownership, it is among the best in the amount of accessible beach. The Sonoma Coast State Beach is under the jurisdiction of the California State Parks' system, and includes most of the ocean shoreline from the Sonoma County line north to Fort Ross State Park above the mouth of the Russian River. The Pinnacle Gulch Trail is the southernmost access to the coast in Sonoma County and leads to a relatively remote and lightly used beach.

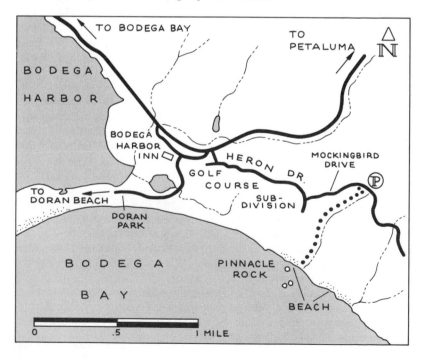

Take CA-1 to Bodega Bay, and turn left into the Bodega Harbour subdivision just before you reach Bodega Bay. Enter the subdivision on South Harbor Way, and immediately take a left on Heron Drive. Continue for just less than a mile to Mockingbird Drive, take another left, and then a left into the parking lot for the trail. The trailhead is just across the street from the parking lot.

Everyone can learn new things by close inspection of plants.

The trail descends gently through a narrow gulch toward the beach, with heavy coastal scrub covering most of the sides of the gulch. This growth is home to numerous birds and small animals, plus larger animals such as raccoon, bobcat, and deer. While bobcat are normally nocturnal animals that seldom venture out into open areas during the day, I have seen them on the hillsides here twice in one year, and heard territorial disputes between males at least three more times.

 Beware of several large areas of poison oak alongside the trail.

Spring is a beautiful time along the Sonoma coast, and the grasslands above the coastal scrub here are full of blooms from February through June.

The trail drops quickly down to the beach at about 0.5 mile. At low tide you can venture about 0.5 mile to the south, and all the way to Doran Beach to the northwest, but beware of incoming tides and high waves that can cut you off from the trail if you venture too far.

There are limited tide pools here, but during extremely low tides many of the large rocks that jut up out of the surf during high tides offer little ones a chance to explore some of the sea life that lives in the intertidal zone.

The narrow beach at the mouth of the gulch is generally protected from cold winds and is a good picnicking site year-round.

58. Bodega Head Loop

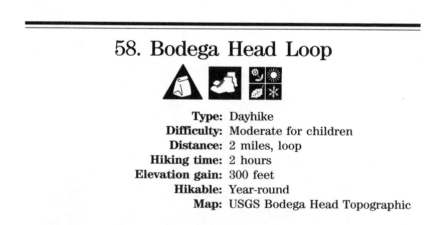

Type: Dayhike
Difficulty: Moderate for children
Distance: 2 miles, loop
Hiking time: 2 hours
Elevation gain: 300 feet
Hikable: Year-round
Map: USGS Bodega Head Topographic

The San Andreas Fault cuts in from the Pacific Ocean to cross under land just to the east of Bodega Head. It was on this very spot that PG&E decided to build a nuclear power plant in the 1950s. Environmentalists and others concerned with the safety of a nuclear plant sitting directly over a major earthquake fault successfully stopped construction of the plant, but only after the utility had dug a large hole that now sits full of spring water. The headlands are now part of the Sonoma Coast State Beach system. This narrow point of land juts out into the ocean, and is exposed to the severe winds and rain that often hit the coast during the winter. As a result, there is very little growth on the head other than low coastal scrub and grasses. These are, however, home to many small birds, and wildflowers bloom profusely in the open areas from February through June. Whale watching from the cliffs overlooking the ocean is also a favorite pastime during the fall and spring migration of the gray whale.

Driving north from Bodega Bay on CA-1, turn left on Bay Flat Road. Continue on Bay Flat for 4 miles to the west parking lot at the top of Bodega Head.

From the west parking lot, head toward the ocean, and the wind-swept sandstone cliffs that offer some of the best whale watching along the Pacific coast. The cliffs along the headlands are dangerous because they are crumbly and unstable. No one should attempt to climb on them or walk along the extreme edge.

Climb over the large logs that mark the limit of the parking lot, and head in a general southerly direction. The trail leads you around the edge of a small cove with a pocket beach that is inaccessible. The kelp beds here often offer sanctuary to sea lions and harbor seals because they feed on the small marine animals that live in the kelp forests.

A lonely, gnarled cypress stands sentinel in the middle of the open

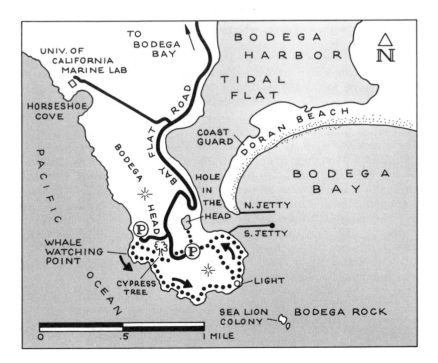

grassland just in from the cliffs at about 0.25 mile. The trail along this portion moves away from the edge and broadens. This is especially welcome for those who fear heights or have overeager children.

At about 0.5 mile, several inviting ledges offer good overlooks for the rocks that jut up from the surf below. Care should be taken when walking out to them, however, since the sandstone cliffs have a tendency to create overhangs as the wind and rain sculpt them. These can break off without warning with the added weight of hikers. All along this section of the trail there are wildflowers in bloom during the spring, and a wildflower guide of the Pacific coast can be very useful if you wish to identify the many blooming plants.

CAUTION

For the next 0.5 mile, the trail reaches the southern point of the headlands, and you can view the entrance to Tomales Bay and Point Reyes Point to the south. The plant cover here begins to turn to coastal scrub from open grassland, and the low-lying wildflowers of the open grassland give way to bushy stands of blue and yellow lupine.

The trail continues along the edge of the cliffs through coastal scrub, and at about 0.75 mile a small island appears off the shore to the south. This is the home of many sea lions, whose barks echo off the cliffs most days. If you have binoculars this is a good spot to stop for a rest and observe the antics of the sea lions as they alternately sun and swim. Have your children imitate the barking sea lions and try to get a response. Have them watch as two or more sea lions try to occupy a choice, sunny spot on the rocks, and guess which one will be the winner of the ensuing struggle.

Just past the spot where you observe the sea lions is a large Coast Guard beacon. There are a number of trails that split off soon after it. Most lead off to the left, and take you back over the ridge to the east parking lot above the "Hole in the Head." If you continue straight ahead, you will follow the contour of the headlands around on an ill-defined trail that offers good views of Bodega Bay, its breakwater, and the Bodega Harbour subdivision. This trail also ends up at the east parking lot.

After a side trip of about 100 yards to view the duck pond that was meant to be the foundation pit for the nuclear power plant, continue through the east parking lot to the trail that is easily seen as it crosses the open grassland toward the cypress tree mentioned earlier.

You may want to stop and let the children explore the sheltered cave formed by the intertwined branches of the windswept tree. On windy days it provides a good shelter for picnickers.

The trail continues back to the west parking lot, which is also the starting point for the next hike.

59. Bodega Head to Dunes Trail

Type: Dayhike
Difficulty: Difficult for children
Distance: 5 miles, round trip
Hiking time: 3 hours
Elevation gain: 600 feet
Hikable: Year-round
Map: USGS Bodega Head Topographic

North of Bodega Head lies a large expanse of sand dunes that once filled Bodega Bay with silt as winter winds moved the massive dunes southward. For many years the movement of the dunes has been stabilized with exotic plants that hold the sand during the windy season. These dunes are a striking contrast to the granitic and sandstone cliffs of Bodega Head, and the views of them as you take this trail north over open grassland are outstanding. Large numbers of deer, some signs of coyote and bobcat, and numerous small birds are all present along the trail.

Just past Bodega Bay on CA-1 turn left on Bay Flat Road. Continue on Bay Flat for 4 miles to the parking lot at the top of Bodega Head.

Head north out of the west parking lot, pass the side trail that leads down to a small pocket beach, and climb through fields of ice plant, an exotic South African plant that often starves out native plants of the area.

The climb is steady, and shortly after you pass the fields of ice plant there is a well-worn trail that leads out to the eroded cliffs. The main trail continues to climb for about another 0.25 mile before it levels out and offers excellent views of the rocky coastline. As you walk through large clumps of bush lupine there is a fork in the trail. For an outstanding view of Horseshoe Cove take the left fork for about 0.25 mile to the overlook. The University of California Marine Laboratory sits on the opposite side of the cove and the dunes spread out beyond. This overlook is also an excellent site for whale watching, and is much less crowded than the cliffs near the parking lot.

Return to the main trail and turn left to continue the hike to the dunes. This is a good spot to head back to the parking lot, however, if anyone in your party is too tired to continue.

At just less than 1 mile you begin a gradual descent and pass by a grove of eucalyptus trees in a canyon to the right. At 1 mile the descent steepens, and the trail reaches the boundaries of the Marine Lab Reserve. Please stay on the trail as you cross the reserve.

The trail then leaves the road to the left and heads north as a narrow track. The trail recrosses the Marine Lab road and heads through more coastal scrub, primarily bush lupine, and descends along the nearly straight line where the coastal scrub/grassland meets the vegetation of the dunes.

The trail soon turns left and generally follows the boundary of the two plant communities. At about 1.25 miles you turn right into the dunes, and round, green posts mark the trail path to the beach. This section of the trail takes you through the highest dunes in the area, and at about 1.5 miles you begin to climb toward the 160-foot dune that is the tallest in the park.

At about 2 miles you pass through a stile and enter state park land. Soon after there is a trail junction. Take the trail straight ahead for the shortest route to the beach. It soon reaches the top of a saddle that overlooks the dunes, beach, and ocean.

Continue winding through the dunes until you reach Salmon Creek Beach, where you can take a rest, watch the shorebirds, and maybe even nap before returning to the trailhead.

The cliffs of Bodega Head are rugged and dangerous.

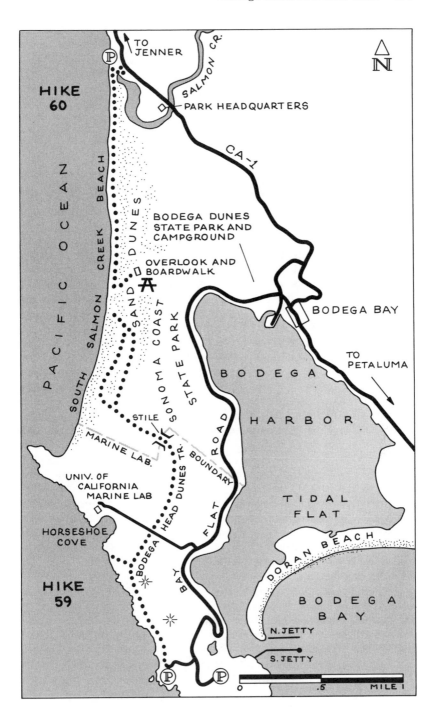

60. Salmon Creek Hike

Type: Dayhike
Difficulty: Moderate for children
Distance: 4 miles, round trip
Hiking time: 2 hours
Elevation gain: 100 feet
Hikable: Year-round
Map: USGS Bodega Head Topographic

While most beaches along the Sonoma coast are small, intimate beaches with little hiking room, Salmon Creek is a long, flat beach that offers several miles of hiking on hard sand between the dunes and the water. There is little variety on this hike, but the wild beauty of the ocean and the numerous seabirds that flit and fly about more than make up for the lack of variation. On summer weekends the beach is crowded near the parking lot, but even then the crowds quickly fall behind as you hike down the beach toward Bodega Head. The crowds seldom materialize after summer has passed, and the best hiking season is fall when the fogs are far out in the ocean, the winds are calm, and the temperature is moderate. Summer fogs are welcome to hikers who live inland where the temperatures rise near 100.

Drive north on CA-1 past Bodega Bay. About 1 mile past the entrance to the Bodega Dunes Campground you will cross over Salmon Creek and pass the Salmon Creek Ranger Station. Go about 0.25 mile farther and the parking lot for the beach is on the left. The parking lot is on a cliff about 100 feet above the beach, and several trails lead from the lot down to the beach.

A lagoon forms at the mouth of Salmon Creek each summer when the water flow becomes too slow to break through the buildup of sand from the pounding waves. Begin your hike by skirting around the lagoon and head toward Bodega Head in the distance. More than 70 kinds of birds have been spotted on or near the lagoon, and birdwatching is good all along the beach.

Dunes begin building up between the lagoon and the sea within 0.25 mile, and grow larger as you continue south. Please stay off them; they are protected because indigenous wildflowers are fragile, and the exotic grasses are needed to hold the dunes in place and keep them out of Bodega Bay to the south.

Two miles down the beach there is a weathered-wood overlook that is the terminus of a boardwalk that crosses the dunes from the Dunes

Campground. This is an excellent place to stop and have a picnic if the winds are not blowing too hard off the ocean. Otherwise, you may want to hike the 0.5 mile or so into the campgrounds, where there are protected picnic tables. This walk will also take you through a section of the dunes so you can observe the plant life there.

It's fun to tempt fate with small waves, but beware of large ones.

61. Kortum Trail—Shell Beach to Blind Beach Trail

Type:	Dayhike
Difficulty:	Moderate for children
Distance:	4 miles, round trip
Hiking time:	2 hours
Elevation gain:	400 feet
Hikable:	Year-round
Map:	USGS Duncan Mills Topographic

Along the Sonoma coast there has been a gentle uplifting of the shore for over 100,000 years. On the average the shore has risen about 1 inch every 100 years as the Pacific and North American plates collide. As a result of this geological movement, sloping terraces that were once covered by waves now sit high above incoming tides as grass-covered terraces that offer ideal hikes for those who like to watch wild waves crash against the rocky shoreline and wonder as raptors soar overhead in search of rodent dinners. Heading north from Shell Beach along the terraces, the constant grazing of cattle for more than 100 years has left the area devoid of most of the native plants that are found to the south

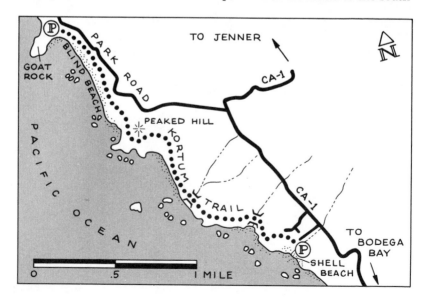

The Kortum Trail leads past secluded, isolated beaches.

of the beach. Grazing has been banned from the terraces to the south for about a decade and native plants have recovered dramatically in that time. The absence of a heavy scrub cover to the north, however, makes it possible to examine the geology of the marine terraces.

Drive north on CA-1 past Bodega Bay for about 7 miles to the Shell Beach parking lot, which is on the west side of the highway.

The Kortum Trail leads out of the parking lot near the trail to the beach and heads north through about 0.25 mile of terrace that has not been grazed for the past decade; it is covered with thick natural coastal scrub. At about 0.25 mile, the trail crosses a fence via a hiker's ladder and turns toward the bluff where it follows a creek. The trail crosses a small bridge at about 0.5 mile and jogs around the head of a large ravine. Just beyond the ravine the trail crosses another hiker's ladder and heads across heavily grazed grassland.

A 0.75-mile side trail leads down to a small rocky beach (be careful if you take this side trip) that is only accessible at low tide.

At about 1 mile the trail descends into a gulch whose sides reveal exposed layers of rounded, ocean-polished pebbles that were once on the ocean floor. The gulch is covered with thick clumps of coast scrub, and a small bridge crosses the creek that drains the gulch.

After you climb out of the gulch the trail passes across level terrace and offers good views of six large stacks of rock just offshore. At 1.2 miles, it crosses another small creek that has several ponds during the wet season. Another tall stack appears offshore, and this one—Gull Rock—is the nesting site for Brandt's cormorants, western gulls, and pigeon guillemots.

Buttercups and irises add color during spring and early summer to the grasslands along this section of the trail that runs alongside the edge of the bluffs. The trail begins to climb and turn inland at 1.3 miles and then descends into a small gully where there is an immense sea stack that shelters a variety of coastal flowers and scrub plants.

The trail climbs out of the gully, and leads to a rock outcropping at 1.5 miles. From there it climbs gently, and goes over another hiker's ladder at about 1.75 miles. Soon afterward the trail approaches the 377-foot summit of Peaked Hill. From this windswept peak you can see for miles to both the north and south along the rugged coast. The trail to the top of the peak is lightly marked, but there is no way to get lost.

Continue for another 0.25 mile to the parking lot for Blind Beach. If some of the little ones are tired, the beach is a good place to rest while the driver returns to Shell Beach for the car. Otherwise, return on the same route, and have a picnic at Shell Beach, which has excellent tide pools at low tide.

62. Shell Beach to Pomo Canyon Trail

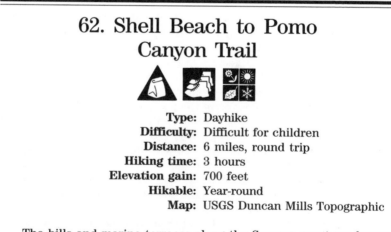

Type: Dayhike
Difficulty: Difficult for children
Distance: 6 miles, round trip
Hiking time: 3 hours
Elevation gain: 700 feet
Hikable: Year-round
Map: USGS Duncan Mills Topographic

The hills and marine terraces along the Sonoma coast are barren and windy places that always seem to have a gray quality, but this changes just over the first ridge from the ocean. There large stands of fir and redwood may grow in sheltered canyons that are drained by seasonal creeks that offer idyllic picnicking sites. The hike from Shell Beach to

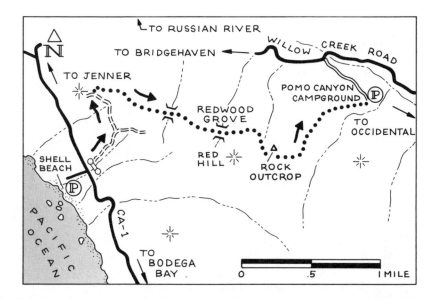

Pomo Canyon Campground leads you through a variety of plant communities that are common to the coastal zone inland from the salt-laden winds that keep larger plants from growing.

Follow directions for hike 61, Kortum Trail, to Shell Beach parking lot. The trailhead to Pomo Canyon Campground is across CA-1 from the parking lot.

The trail follows an old ranch road for about 0.5 mile up to the top of the first ridge. The views of the coast are spectacular as you take rest stops. From this side of the ridge you can see south to Point Reyes Point and north past the mouth of the Russian River. Irises and other colorful, low-lying wildflowers dot the hillsides here during the spring, and raptors often drift low over the ridge on windy updrafts off the ocean.

As you reach the ridge several trails converge; take the fork straight ahead. It is marked by a small redwood signpost. For the next 0.75 mile the trail (still the old ranch road) makes a number of short ups and downs as it winds through meadows, over spring-fed seepages, and along the contours of the hillside. The views of Jenner and the mouth of the Russian River are excellent along this stretch.

At about 1.5 miles from the trailhead, you will come to a hiker's ladder. Climb over the fence and take a hard right. The trail continues along the fence line, climbing gradually for about 0.5 mile. Plenty of berries grow along this section of the trail, but if you decide to do some picking, be careful because poison oak abounds here also. The views to the north are breathtaking.

At just less than 2 miles you come to the first of two groves of trees

There is easy hiking along the trail to Pomo Canyon from Shell Beach.

that have creeks running out of them down the hillside. While the first is inviting and is a good place to stop if you need a rest, the second, just up the trail, is really an enchanted forest, complete with a wooden bridge you can sit on while you rest or snack. This is a good turnaround spot if any hikers are tired, but the trail is relatively level for the next 0.25 mile, where you cross a small creek, go around a very bushy bay tree, and come to a wonderful rock outcropping that is easy to climb. From the top you can see several forested ridges to the north, part of the Russian River Valley, and the Willow Creek drainage area.

From the rock outcropping the trail begins to descend to Pomo Canyon Campground. Immediately past the large outcropping is a creek that is dry by midsummer, but rumbles down the hillside during and after the rainy season. The trail soon passes another group of rocks, and then heads into a forest of Douglas fir that have been battered and bent by centuries of powerful coastal winds. Gnarled and drooping bay are also near the side of the trail, and in at least one instance, over it.

At about 2.5 miles there is an old Douglas fir beside the trail that is at least 8 feet in diameter. Soon afterward the trail enters a grove of redwoods and drops into the campground.

There are picnic sites at the campground and open grassland near the creek. You can return to Shell Beach after a rest, or you can have a shuttle vehicle parked at the campground for a one-way hike.

63. Black Ranch Trail

Type: Dayhike
Difficulty: Difficult for children
Distance: 3.5 miles, round trip
Hiking time: 2 hours
Elevation gain: 600 feet
Hikable: Year-round
Map: USGS Duncan Mills Topographic

Along the coast above Jenner, where the Russian River enters the Pacific, rugged cliffs rise as high as 1300 feet above the ocean. These offer panoramic views of the coast, but few access routes down to the ocean. The wildflowers that cling to the steep sides of these cliffs are abundant and colorful during the spring bloom, and the rugged terrain along the few trails that do venture down to the sea is well worth investigating.

Follow CA-1 north of Jenner for about 3 miles. The parking area for Black Ranch is on the west side of the highway just past Russian Gulch State Park at the junction of CA-1 and Meyers Grade Road.

Three trails lead out of the Black Ranch Trailhead. The first is a 1-mile paved loop that is accessible to handicapped hikers; the second is

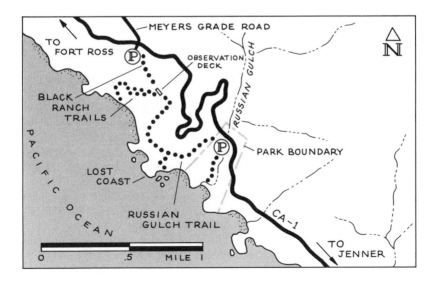

a 2.75-mile steep round trip to the beach, and the third is the 3.5-mile round trip to Russian Gulch. All head east on the asphalt trail out of the gravel parking lot. The paved trail gently descends along the top of the rolling grasslands, and at just under 0.5 mile there is an observation platform on top of a small hill where there are views from Fort Ross to the north to Point Reyes to the south. The trail continues at a gradual climb, and at about 0.75 mile there is another observation point.

The paved trail ends here, and a dirt trail follows an old coast wagon road as it descends toward the Lost Coast. After several switchbacks that bring the trail to the top of the 200-foot cliffs above Lost Coast (at about 1.25 miles) the trail to the isolated beach at Lost Coast heads off to the right. The descent down to the beach is steep. The left fork of the trail

continues along the top of the bluffs to about 1.5 miles, and then drops down to the parking lot at Russian Gulch at 1.75 miles.

Return by the same route, or have a shuttle vehicle at Russian Gulch.

There are a number of other new trails along this section of the coast, and all are worth exploring.

64. Pioneer/East Ridge Trails Loop

Type: Dayhike
Difficulty: Moderate for children
Distance: 3 miles, loop
Hiking time: 2 hours
Elevation gain: 400 feet
Hikable: Year-round
Map: USGS Guerneville Topographic

Redwoods are awe-inspiring trees that stand high above all else, and groves of virgin trees are few in northern California. The wood in the large old trees was just too valuable for most lumbermen to ignore. But this grove of virgin trees in Armstrong Redwoods State Reserve was saved through the efforts of one investor and lumberman, Colonel James Armstrong, who came to California in 1874 to invest in the lumber industry. He became enthralled with the ancient grove of giants along Fife Creek just north of Guerneville and attempted to save them from destruction. Even after his death in 1900, his family pursued his work, and in 1917 the grove became a county park. The state parks' system acquired the land in 1934, and today it is one of the finest groves of virgin trees in the lower Redwood Empire region.

Take the CA-116 exit off US 101 at Cotati and head west through
Sebastopol, continuing another 16 miles to Guerneville. Head straight at
the four-way stop in Guerneville and go another 2.2 miles to the park
entrance. Park there and walk in.

The Southern Pomo Indian tribe had many villages in the region
surrounding Armstrong Grove, but avoided the grove of redwoods, which
they called "the dark hole." They thought the dark, damp, and cool forest
was inhabited by evil spirits. Today visitors come to the grove to experience the primeval and untamed feelings that emanate from the silent
surroundings. The tall trees, rushing torrents of water in midwinter, and
the muted colors of wildflowers in spring all help hikers gain this experience.

From the park entrance begin your hike along the main road into
the park, and veer left after about 200 yards. The trail passes the Parson
Jones Tree, which at 310 feet is the tallest tree in the grove, and turns
to the right after about 75 feet. Numbered posts along the trail are keyed
to a nature guide that you can pick up at park headquarters.

The trail continues through a mixed redwood and fir forest that
includes bay, tanoaks, and big-leafed maple. At just less than 0.5 mile,
the giant Colonel Armstrong Tree (just a couple of feet shorter than the
Parson Jones Tree) stands out ahead of you. With a diameter of almost
15 feet, this is the most massive tree in the park.

There are a large number of old redwood trees along this stretch
of trail that have large caverns at their bases formed by scars left from
long-ago fires. Children love to play in these and pretend they are trolls
and other mythical forest creatures.

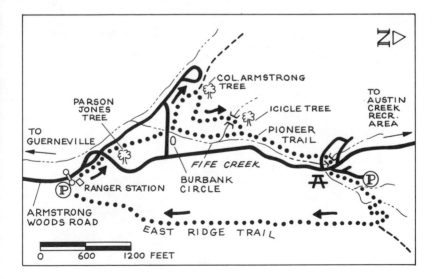

The trail forks at the base of the Armstrong Tree, and the left fork heads off into the Austin Creek State Recreation Area as the Pool Ridge Trail. Take the right fork, which slowly descends and curves around the base of the hillside. After following alongside Fife Creek, the trail comes to a junction with many trails. Keep to the far left trail for a less crowded walk along the nature trail.

At about 0.75 mile you cross a footbridge and immediately face the Icicle Tree. The Icicle Tree has large growths coming out from its base that early loggers thought were shaped like icicles. Have the children try to guess what made these formations, and then read the explanation on the plaque by the base of the tree.

The path soon ends as it joins the Pioneer Trail. This is a good turnaround for those who are not interested in going farther, because the right path heads back to the parking lot through an area with many wildflowers indigenous to the redwood forest.

Streams that run through redwood groves make good rest stops.

To continue the longer loop, turn left and keep along the trail beside the creek. After crossing several small bridges, you will come to the picnic area at 1 mile. This is a good place to rest and snack.

Past the picnic area veer right on the paved road and veer right again on a paved trail. You will soon come to restrooms and a parking lot. At the east end of the parking lot head up the East Ridge Trail.

For the next 0.5 mile, the trail climbs up switchbacks through a mixed forest to a junction at the top of the ridge. Take the right fork and hike along the ridge, where you will notice the difference in vegetation because the shallow soil here supports mostly hardwoods with an occasional Douglas fir. The trail goes up and down along this section, with views over the redwood grove to the left.

At about 2.25 miles, the trail begins a steep descent of the west slope of the ridge, and soon reenters the redwood forest below. The trail leads through smaller redwoods with thick batches of huckleberry.

At about 3 miles you reach the parking lot.

65. Austin Creek/Gilliam Creek Trail Loop

Type: Dayhike
Difficulty: Difficult for children
Distance: 4 miles, loop
Hiking time: 3 hours
Elevation gain: 800 feet
Hikable: Year-round
Map: USGS Guerneville Topographic

Although Austin Creek State Recreation Area is adjacent to Armstrong Redwood Grove it stands in stark contrast to the cool, shaded canyon where the redwoods thrive. The open grasslands of the rolling to steep hills in the recreation area are emerald green after the winter rains, but turn to a golden brown as the heat of summer comes. And the heat does come. While visitors come to Armstrong Grove to enjoy the cool comfort during the summer, the hills of Austin Creek bake in some of the hottest weather in the region. This makes spring and fall the best times to hike here, although winter hikes can be pleasant after a dry spell. Summer hikes are best done during cool, foggy times.

Follow the directions for hike 61 to Armstrong Grove, enter the park,

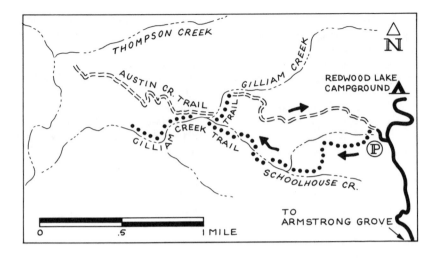

and go past the picnic area. Continue for a little over 1.5 miles to a fork in the road. Go left to the parking area for Gilliam Creek Trail.

This trail descends through a mixed forest of hardwoods and fir, with an occasional redwood, toward the headwaters of Schoolhouse Creek. The descent is steep for the first 0.25 mile, then it levels out and climbs gently for a short distance. It again descends toward a seasonal creek. Just before the creek there is a fine rock outcropping.

At about 0.5 mile, the trail enters a broad expanse of flat grassland that affords excellent views of the ridges between Austin Creek and the ocean 14 miles away. It crosses the lower part of the meadow and fords another seasonal creek. From there the trail again climbs to another meadow where the serpentine slopes of Red Slide and the ridge above it known as The Cedars come into view.

The trail begins to descend Gilliam Ridge at about 0.75 mile, passes by some large oaks, and crosses a fork of Schoolhouse Creek at about 1 mile. From there it crosses other branches of the creek and winds through woods and meadows. The trail soon begins a steeper descent as it follows the creek and then levels out at a section where there are exposed veins of dark brown and green serpentine. Near 1.25 miles the trail rounds a big bend and crosses a fork of Schoolhouse Creek where there are large, moss-covered boulders. This is a good place to stop for a short rest and exploration of the creek.

Just after 1.5 miles you come to the confluence of Schoolhouse Creek and its major tributary, and the trail continues to descend along the creek. After fording the creek several times, you pass a large black oak tree and reach a junction near Gilliam Creek just past 2 miles.

Go right at this junction, fording Schoolhouse Creek once again, and follow Gilliam Creek Trail upstream for about 1.5 miles to a fire road.

This stretch of trail offers chances to explore small ponds with fish and rapids that tumble over rocks in the creek. Many types of ferns and mosses are also found along the creek.

The climb up Gilliam Creek is steep, and you will find yourself exploring more and more, and hiking less and less, and when you turn right on the fire road be prepared for another steep ascent.

The road takes you back to the trailhead.

---

66. Ragle Ranch Trail Loop

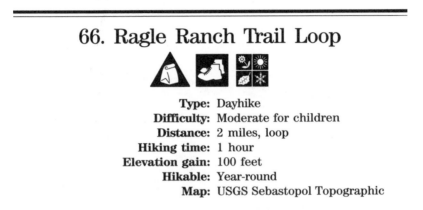

Type: Dayhike
Difficulty: Moderate for children
Distance: 2 miles, loop
Hiking time: 1 hour
Elevation gain: 100 feet
Hikable: Year-round
Map: USGS Sebastopol Topographic

Ragle Ranch Regional Park has the appearance of any well-groomed suburban park with its green lawns and playing fields, but there is more to the park than that. Behind the green facade lies an undeveloped part where hikers can explore wetlands and riparian habitats that are home to dozens of species of birds. Signs of coyote, badger, raccoon, and opossum can also be found along the trail as it crosses open grassland, oak woodland, and creekside growth. The latter provides both home and food for much of the wildlife.

Take the CA-116 exit off US 101 and continue to downtown Sebastopol. Turn west on Bodega Avenue and go just over a mile to Ragle Road. Turn right on Ragle; the park entrance is 0.5 mile on the left. Park at the first parking area. The trail begins at the green gate along the fence to the west of the gazebo.

Pass through the gate, and head downhill through an old orchard area. This section is home to many field birds such as the meadowlark, and various raptors soar overhead.

At about 0.25 mile, you reach an area that is very muddy in the winter after the rains, with a small bridge that crosses the worst of the wetland. Several hundred yards past the first footbridge is Atascadero Creek, which is crossed by a larger bridge. This creek is often dry by the end of summer, but the thick growth on its banks creates wonderful places for children to explore.

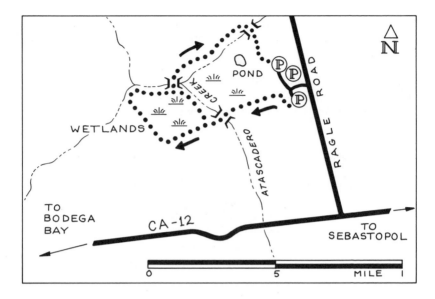

The trail splits just after the bridge, with one fork going to the right and one straight ahead. The one to the right follows the creek and cuts about 0.5 mile off your hike.

Continue straight ahead and you come to another wet area with a large grove of weeping willow on the left. The limbs grow close to the ground and form a canopy that your children can play under. The trail continues around the western boundary of the park, circling a large meadow that is very soggy in the wet season. At about 1 mile the trail begins to descend gently and enters a small grove of oak.

About 200 yards past the oaks the trail approaches the banks of Atascadero Creek in another wet area. Several openings in the dense brush allow access to the creek along here. At 1.25 miles you come to a normally dry tributary of Atascadero that drains the vast meadow. This can be a wet crossing after heavy rains, but generally it is possible to cross without getting wet.

The trail rejoins the right fork at 1.5 miles, and turns left over another bridge across Atascadero Creek. It veers to the right as it approaches a vineyard and passes a grove of eucalyptus on the left. Scattered oaks grow above the edge of the wetlands along this section, which is a wintering site for waterfowl.

There are more access points to the creek along this section of the trail, and you come to another bridge at a little over 1.75 miles. As you cross over the bridge look closely on your right and you will see a lightly used trail that leads into the trees. Just a few yards off the trail is a small

Gnarly oaks are only one attraction of parks in the North Bay.

pond that is home to a multitude of small water animals during the wet season, and it makes an excellent hidden picnic area in the summer.

The trail soon comes to another green gate. Pass through it and head up the paved road to the parking lot.

67. Santa Rosa/Sebastopol Multiuse Trail

Type:	Dayhike
Difficulty:	Moderate for children
Distance:	4 miles, round trip
Hiking time:	2 hours
Elevation gain:	Level
Hikable:	Year-round
Map:	USGS Sebastopol Topographic

There has been a movement across the nation to reclaim abandoned railroad rights-of-way as multiuse trails for hikers, bikers, and horseback riders. Over 500 such conversions have occurred in the past several decades, and one was along the railway that once ran from Santa Rosa to Forestville. As the rails were removed from the right-of-way, the Sonoma County Parks Department began the process of converting more than 20

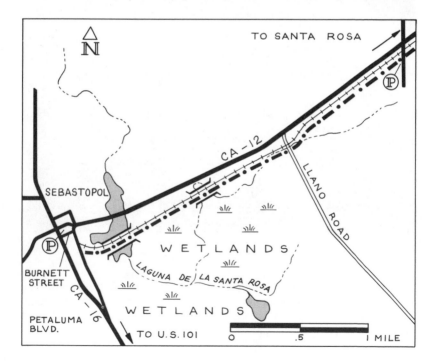

The railroad has given way to hikers along the Santa Rosa/Sebastopol Multiuse Trail.

miles of this right-of-way to a multiuse trail. This has included paving 9 feet of the right-of-way with asphalt to make it a year-round trail. As of late 1991, 3 miles of the trail had been completed between Sebastopol and Merced Avenue near Santa Rosa.

Take the CA-116 exit off US 101 and continue to downtown Sebastopol. Just before the first stoplight in Sebastopol, take a left on Burnett Street and park in the city parking lot. Follow the exit out the east end of the parking lot. The trail begins across Petaluma Boulevard.

Although the trail begins amidst commercial residential buildings in Sebastopol it soon enters an undeveloped portion of the Laguna de la Santa Rosa, a large wetland area that is being considered for designation as a national wildlife refuge since it is the largest remaining wetland along the north coast.

At about 0.25 mile, the trail crosses the first of several old railroad bridges. This bridge crosses the main stream of the laguna, and is a good lookout post for those interested in watching crawdads and other small water animals.

Past the bridge the vegetation on both sides of the trail thins out and to the south there is open grassland that is irrigated by treated effluent from the Santa Rosa sewage treatment plant. This area is home to many birds, and is covered with yellow mustard blossoms during the spring. Other wildflowers can be seen along the trail.

The trail crosses another bridge at about 0.75 mile. Large clumps of teasels, a thistle-like plant with prickly seed pods that grows in disturbed areas, grow on the north side of the trail at about 1 mile.

The trail comes to another populated area near 2 miles, and crosses Llano Road there. This is a good turnaround point, but those who want to walk farther can continue for another mile to the end of the paved trail at Merced Avenue.

Return on the same trail to Sebastopol.

177

68. Woodland Ridge Loop

Type: Dayhike
Difficulty: Moderate for children
Distance: 1.5 miles, loop
Hiking time: 1 hour
Elevation gain: 150 feet
Hikable: Year-round
Map: USGS Healdsburg Topographic

The U.S. Army Corps of Engineers built Warm Springs Dam, which impounds Lake Sonoma, in the 1980s after years of political maneuvering by both opponents and proponents. While the rationale given for building the dam may have been suspect, the fact that miles of excellent hiking trails have been developed around the lake is indisputable. These trails take hikers into little used sections of the rolling to steep hills, and offer both long and short hikes through a variety of habitats. Wild turkey, feral hogs, black-tailed deer, and coyote are some of the larger animals that can be seen along the trails, and dozens of species of small birds live in the forests and open grassland. A number of the trails lead to hike-in campsites that are seldom full and offer good access to the lake for those who like to fish. The Woodland Ridge Loop serves as an excellent introduction to the many types of plants that grow in the Lake Sonoma region.

Take the Dry Creek Road exit off US 101 in Healdsburg, then head west. Continue for about 12 miles to the fish hatchery and visitor center. The Woodland Ridge Loop begins at the far end of the visitor center parking lot.

Near the picnic area south of the parking lot there is a large map of the Woodland Ridge Trail Loop. Head past the map into a small grove of redwood trees and turn left.

The trail goes up a number of steps made of redwood (some say 63—have the children count them. Is 63 right?) out of the redwood grove into a forest of large bay trees. After the trail reaches the end of the steps, it again enters a redwood grove, this time one of young trees sprouting out of decaying stumps of old redwoods that were cut years ago. The climb eases off here and begins a contour around the hill. This section of the trail goes through a mixed forest.

As the trail reaches another set of steps, it begins a steady climb, and at about 0.25 mile passes by some large Douglas fir (as large as 4 feet in diameter). Soon afterward the forest thins and the trail levels out as it passes along a ridge with scattered oak and manzanita. The Mayacamas Range is visible to the east, with Geyser Peak to the north and Mount St. Helena to the south. On cool days you can see the steam from the geysers condensing as it rises.

Four different kinds of oak (coast live oak, canyon live oak, interior live oak, and black oak) grow along the ridge. Have the children look for the four different types of leaves. The coast, canyon, and interior live oak all have very similar leaves, although the coast live oak leaves are more rounded than the other two, which are oblong, 1 to 4 inches long, and up to 1 inch wide, with spiny tips on the small lobes. These three trees are also evergreens. The black oak is the only deciduous tree among the four, and its leaves are larger (4 to 8 inches long and up to 4 inches wide), and much more deeply lobed.

At about 0.5 mile you encounter several large madrone that shade the trail. These have profuse white blooms in the spring that stand out against the green hillside that is dappled by swatches of red, yellow, and

The whole group wants to investigate an interesting object.

blue wildflowers. The trail reaches its highest point shortly afterward, and you have good views of Alexander and Dry Creek valleys to the east.

As you descend, you'll see a glimpse of Lake Sonoma. At 0.75 mile the trail forks. Take the left fork for a short side trip to an observation point where you overlook the visitor center, fish hatchery, Warm Springs Dam, and Lake Sonoma.

Return to the fork and continue downhill. After going through a mixed fir and oak forest, you suddenly descend into a thick, dark grove of beautiful madrone. This is one of the best stands of madrone in the region, and the tangle of shiny limbs shedding their bark is a sight many children never forget. As the rough, outer bark sheds off the madrone a very smooth, orange bark is left. Hikers often call the madrone the "refrigerator tree" because its smooth bark and dense wood are always cooler than the surrounding air. Have your children knock on a thick limb of the madrone to listen to the sound. Madrone is composed of some of the heaviest, densest wood of any tree in North America, and it emits a sharp sound when hit, rather than a dull thud.

As the trail descends even more steeply the parking lot and visitor center come into view, and the trail emerges into an open grassland with native bunch grasses. The trail descends a series of about 50 steps, passes a water tank, and winds over a bridge to the picnic area.

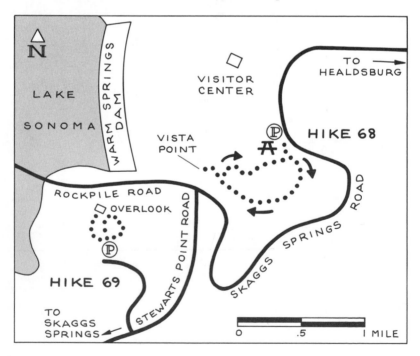

All ages enjoy the offerings at Lake Sonoma.

69. Promontory Trail Loop

Type: Dayhike
Difficulty: Easy for children
Distance: 0.5 mile, loop
Hiking time: 0.5 hour
Elevation gain: Minimal
Hikable: Year-round
Map: USGS Healdsburg Topographic

This short nature trail gives an excellent introduction to the plants of the Lake Sonoma region without requiring a lot of heavy hiking. It adjoins the Promontory Overlook, so a walk along the trail and up to the overlook provides you with an excellent understanding of the land around Lake Sonoma.

Follow directions for hike 68, Woodland Ridge Loop, and continue on past the visitor center to the first road on the left, Stewarts Point Road. Turn left and drive for a little less than 0.5 mile to a turnoff on the right. This road leads you to the South Lake Trailhead and Promontory Overlook. Continue to the end and park near the restrooms. The trail follows the contour of the hill behind the restrooms.

This short trail has 7 marked stations that tell about plant communities of the area. These include information on Native American uses for plants in the area, large birds that may be seen above here, natural recycling systems, Pacific madrone trees, coast redwoods, and live oaks.

After completing the short loop, you can walk out to the end of the overlook adjacent to the trail and view Warm Springs Dam, Lake Sonoma, and the surrounding land.

---

70. No Name Flat/Lone Pine Trail Loop

Type: Dayhike
Difficulty: Difficult for children
Distance: 6 miles, loop
Hiking time: 4 hours
Elevation gain: 600 feet
Hikable: Year-round
Map: USGS Healdsburg Topographic

The land in between the two major arms of Lake Sonoma offers a wide choice for hiking. Rockpile Road divides the area into two separate, distinct areas. To the north of the road most of the land is covered by scrub and chaparral, with an occasional Digger pine standing in sharp contrast to the lower vegetation. The trails through this area head down to the shore of the Dry Creek arm of the lake and lead through country that is heavily populated by feral pigs. There are also many raptors that nest in this region, including the endangered peregrine falcon. Most of the trails are short ones that can be hiked in series to make longer loops. To the south of the road the terrain is more rolling, and there are more oak forests and open grassland.

 Follow the directions for hike 68, Woodland Ridge Loop, and continue past the visitor center. At the fork of Skaggs Springs/Stewarts Point Road and Rockpile Road, just less than 2 miles from the visitor center, stay to the right on Rockpile Road. This takes you over the high bridge at the junction of the two arms of the lake. The parking lot for No Name Flat is about 2.5 miles past the junction (about 0.5 mile past the Digger Pine Flat parking lot on the right).

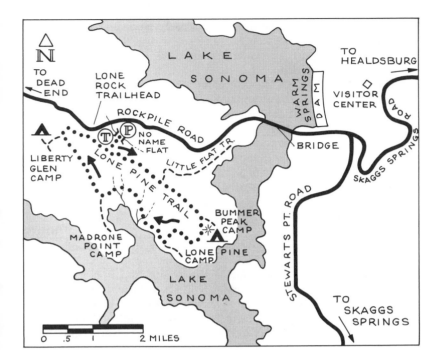

The trail begins at the parking area, veers to the right, and crosses a footbridge over a seasonal creek. From there you begin a gentle climb through open grassland dotted with an occasional oak and buckeye. This hillside is brightened during the spring with dozens of spots of wildflowers. The climb continues for a little over 0.25 mile and then begins to descend slowly. At about 0.5 mile the trail dead ends. Take a left to Bummer Peak.

The trail descends for a short distance, levels off, and then climbs to the top of a ridge that offers great views of the lake and the mountains beyond. The view to the northeast is dominated by Mount St. Helena and the Dry Creek arm of the lake. To the south the slope descends almost 700 feet to the Warm Springs arm of the lake, where the marina is located. This is a good spot for an early break.

At about 1 mile you come to the Little Flat Trail to the left. Continue to the right, and the trail is a series of ups and downs, with the downs much longer than the ups. The oaks gradually disappear and are replaced by Digger pines and toyon bushes. Serpentine outcroppings are located along the trail.

Just past 1.5 miles you enter a large grove of black oak, and in less than 0.25 mile a side trail leads to the top of 1150-foot Bummer Peak. Although the peak is the highest point around the view is limited by the trees.

The Bummer Peak campsite, located near the peak, has tables and restrooms, and is a good stop for lunch or a rest. The view from the campsite of the Warm Springs arm of the lake, complete with several islands, is very panoramic.

The trail heads down after the camp, and at about 2 miles it begins a steep 300-foot descent to the lakeshore. Wildflowers abound here in the spring, standing out in brilliant contrast to the green grasses on the slopes. At about 2.25 miles, the trail levels out and a side trail leads to the Lone Pine Camp, which is only 200 yards away. This is another good place to stop for a picnic if you didn't stop at Bummer Peak.

The main trail continues to parallel the shore and crosses the mouth of a gulch with a seasonal creek that has plenty of water into late spring. At about 2.5 miles you begin a gradual climb away from the lake and cross one good sized and two smaller creeks before the trail levels off in a large meadow.

The junction with the Madrone Point Trail is at about 3 miles. The climb is steady, with only a few level sections, for the next mile. This area is rich with wildflowers during the spring, and is home to wild turkeys, quail, and grouse. You are very likely to hear these birds, and may be lucky enough to see some, as you make the climb.

The trail joins the Liberty Glen Trail at about 4 miles. Go right onto a trail that winds along the contour of the slope through open grassland. It soon meets Rockpile Road at the Lone Rock Trailhead. The trail veers away from the road and gradually descends until it comes to the No Name Flat Trail on the left. From there retrace your route to the parking lot.

One word to the wise. It gets *hot* in the summer in this region, and plenty of fluids should be carried on any hike.

Emerald grass-covered hills overlook an arm of Lake Sonoma.

71. Lake Trail Loop

Type: Dayhike
Difficulty: Moderate for children
Distance: 2 miles, loop
Hiking time: 1 hour
Elevation gain: 300 feet
Hikable: Year-round
Map: USGS Healdsburg or Mark West
Springs Topographic

Foothill Oaks Regional Park is another of the small regional parks that Sonoma County has developed as vast developments have encroached on what was once open land. This one was scheduled to open in Sep-

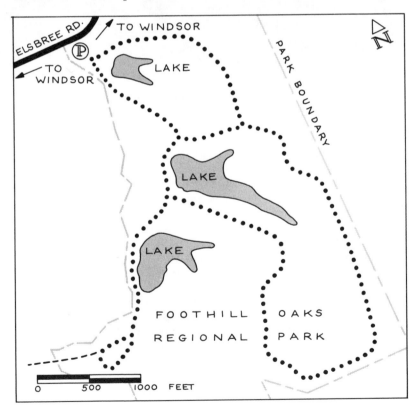

Small birds are found in abundance among the cattails and reeds around lakes.

tember 1991, and trails are currently under construction. The land within the 208-acre park is made up of slightly rolling hills with several small, quiet ponds and scattered groves of coast live oak. The ponds provide excellent places to explore for small water animals such as frogs, and the rushes and cattails around the edges offer food and shelter for many birds and small mammals.

Take the Shiloh Road exit off US 101 north of Santa Rosa. Continue 1 mile east on Shiloh and turn left on Old Redwood Highway. After 3 miles turn right on Lakewood Road and take the first left onto Brooks Road. Go 0.5 mile and turn right on Foothill Road, then take a quick left on Elsbree Road to the park.

Although the trails in Foothill Oaks were unmarked as this guide went to press, there was a rudimentary loop trail that goes for about 2 miles through the oaks and passes by three ponds. Although there is no fishing or swimming in the ponds, you can explore around the edges. The trail is easy, with few steep climbs.

A picnic area, with tables and chemical toilets, is planned near the entrance of the park, as well as a large map of trails.

72. Big Leaf Ridge Loop

Type: Dayhike
Difficulty: Difficult for children
Distance: 4 miles, loop
Hiking time: 3 hours
Elevation gain: 850 feet
Hikable: Year-round
Map: USGS Healdsburg or Mark West Springs Topographic

Shiloh Ranch Regional park is a neighbor of Foothill Oaks and is both larger and more rugged. Sitting on the edge of the Mayacamas Range, the park has grasslands, chaparral, oak, madrone, and fir plant communities. It is rugged canyon country with deep ravines separating sharp ridges. The 350-acre park is home to a number of deer, feral pigs, coyote, fox, and an occasional bobcat. Some even claim there are mountain lions in the park. All of this within a stone's throw of subdivisions and vineyards that can be seen from several vista points along the trail.

Take the Shiloh Road exit off US 101 north of Santa Rosa. Continue on Shiloh Road until it dead ends into Faught Road. Turn right for a long block and then left into the parking lot. The trail begins at the rear of the parking lot.

The Big Leaf Trail climbs up a small hill for several hundred feet where it forks. Take the right fork and gradually climb through an oak forest, where madrone and manzanita are scattered, along with plenty of poison oak. Wildflowers are plentiful here in the spring, with poppies, lupine, buttercups, and brodiaea.

For the next 0.25 mile, the trail is fairly level, and follows the southwest boundary of the park. After it passes an unusual wooden water tank, it begins to climb into a shaded portion of a Douglas fir forest. At about 0.5 mile, it parallels a split redwood fence for a short distance before beginning a steep ascent.

The trail crosses a gulch at about 0.75 mile, and then climbs through a meadow filled with colorful wildflowers in the spring.

The Big Leaf Trail dead ends into the Ridge Trail at about 1 mile. Take a left and climb along a grassy ridge toward the northeast. The trail soon descends slightly, and chaparral covers the hillsides. As the ridge merges with a larger and higher ridge that comes in from the right, it begins to climb again.

Large fir trees stand above the trail as it climbs in and out of two lush ravines before it begins a steady climb toward a large power line tower. Just past the power lines, which are at the halfway point of the hike, the ridge juts out to an overlook that is a good place for a rest stop or picnic. The overlook offers views of the vineyards and Russian River Canyon to the west.

The trail continues down the side of the ravine and crosses the head of it before it begins another steep ascent at about 1.5 miles. After a short, steep climb the trail joins with another from the right. This is the Pond Trail.

Those who do not want to explore farther can keep to the left and head back to the parking area for a 2.5-mile loop.

Others can take the trail to the right and climb a steep section of trail to a large meadow that offers spectacular views of Mount St. Helena to the north and the Santa Rosa Plains to the south.

Even the best have to be assisted at times.

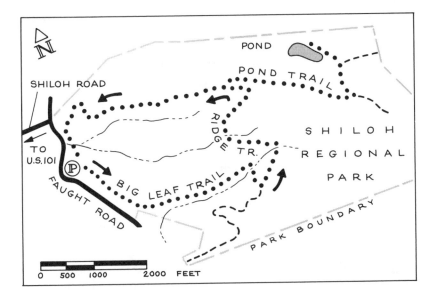

Just under 2 miles the trail begins a gradual, winding descent, and then begins to drop more rapidly. A side trail goes to the left at just over 2 miles, and takes you down a lightly used path to two ponds. These have some willows along their shores, but are mostly bare. This is an excellent place to stop for lunch and a rest.

A path to be completed in 1993 will follow the creek along the boundary of the park to the trailhead, but for now you must backtrack to the junction of Pond and Ridge trails. From there you climb for a short distance before beginning your long descent back to the trailhead.

Return to the junction of Pond and Ridge trails, which is 1.75 miles from the trailhead. From there the trail passes through open grassland, but soon enters chaparral, with some madrone and oak interspersed. After a roller-coaster-like section with several ups and downs, the drop steepens at 2 miles. The trail then leaves the ridge, heads down through an oak forest, and runs along the side of a green canyon filled with birds.

At the bottom of the hill you reach a trail junction. Take a right and return to the parking area.

73. Santa Rosa Creek Trail

Type: Dayhike
Difficulty: Easy for children
Distance: 1 mile, round trip
Hiking time: 1 hour
Elevation gain: Level
Hikable: Year-round
Map: USGS Santa Rosa Topographic

Cities across the country are rediscovering the benefits of having creeks and rivers that are accessible to the general public and that offer residents an opportunity to stroll along a lush creek bank or explore shallow pools of unpolluted water. Santa Rosa has joined this group of aware cities and is in the process of restoring Brush and Santa Rosa creeks within the city limits. Along with this restoration have come creekside trails that offer a quiet walk amidst civilization.

Take the CA-12 exit off US 101 in Santa Rosa. Drive east on CA-12 to Farmers Lane and turn left. Continue on Farmers Lane to Fourth Street and take a right. As you approach the sign for Brush Creek Road, watch for an empty field on the right. Park there. The trail begins to

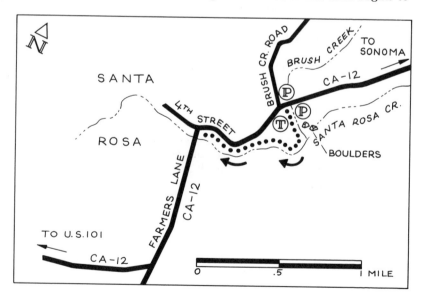

These quiet pools become roaring rapids after winter rains.

the north of the road beneath the bridge that crosses Brush Creek. The gate is to keep vehicles out.

The first section of the trail is along a denuded Brush Creek that is presently full of green algae. This area is being restored, and riparian growth is coming back to protect the creek water from the heat of the midday sun.

The trail fords the creek after several hundred yards (a pedestrian bridge is planned), and the basalt boulders just beyond the ford sit where a future park is planned. During summer and fall the creek makes soothing, tinkling sounds as it passes over the rocks, but it becomes a rapid with waterfalls during the runoff of winter and spring.

Just west of the boulders, Brush and Santa Rosa creeks join. Go right on the footpath along Santa Rosa Creek. Santa Rosa Creek, at least along this section, was never channelized the way Brush Creek was above, and it meanders in a natural manner. The present trail continues for several hundred yards until you are just below CA-12. Future plans are for another footbridge here and an extension of the trail to Farmers Lane, but for now you must retrace your steps back to the parking area.

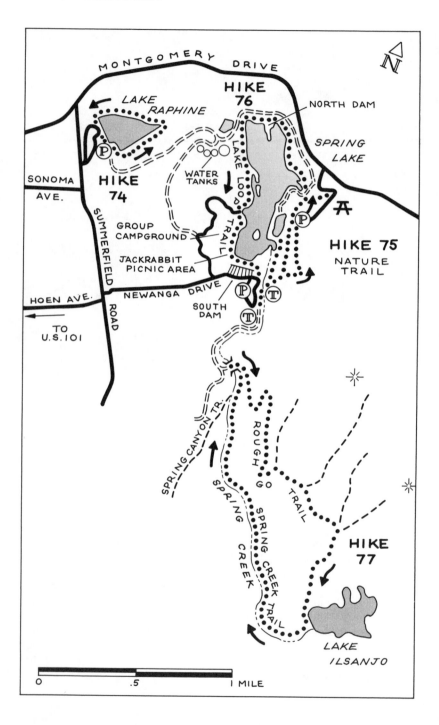

74. Lake Ralphine Loop

Type: Dayhike
Difficulty: Moderate for children
Distance: 1 mile, loop
Hiking time: 1 hour
Elevation gain: Minimal
Hikable: Year-round
Map: USGS Santa Rosa Topographic

Howarth Park is a well-developed city park with tennis courts, softball diamonds, playgrounds, and picnic sites, but it also has Lake Ralphine. This reservoir has stocked trout, boat rides, and hundreds of ducks to feed, plus a loop trail that children love to trek.

Take the CA-12 exit off US 101 in Santa Rosa. Continue on CA-12 to Farmers Lane, where the freeway ends. Turn left, and continue on Farmers Lane to Sonoma Avenue. Turn right on Sonoma Avenue and continue until it dead ends at Summerfield Road. Take a left, and Howarth Park will be on your right. Turn into the park and go to the parking lot at the top of the hill. The trail around Lake Ralphine begins at the east side of the parking lot.

Lake Ralphine sits in the middle of Santa Rosa, yet offers a natural setting.

The trail is paved asphalt for the first 0.25 mile or so, but there are a number of lakeside accesses that wander through the heavy chaparral that covers the south side of the lake. As you reach the east end of the lake, watch for a dirt trail that heads off to the left. This crosses a small creek that feeds the lake and climbs up the far bank of the lake.

From here to the dam at the west end of the lake the trail skirts the contour of the hill, and rambles over tree roots as it leads you close to the water and back up the side of the hill. Many small trails lead down to the water where fishermen have chosen to cast for the trout, bass, and blue gill that populate the lake.

At about 0.75 mile, the trail leads back to the dam. Cross over the dam and return to the picnic area where you can feed the ducks.

75. Nature Trail

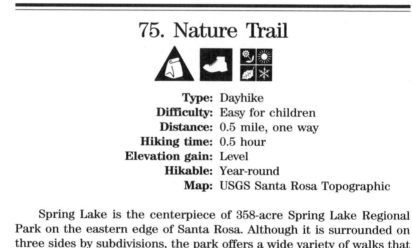

Type: Dayhike
Difficulty: Easy for children
Distance: 0.5 mile, one way
Hiking time: 0.5 hour
Elevation gain: Level
Hikable: Year-round
Map: USGS Santa Rosa Topographic

Spring Lake is the centerpiece of 358-acre Spring Lake Regional Park on the eastern edge of Santa Rosa. Although it is surrounded on three sides by subdivisions, the park offers a wide variety of walks that can be taken year-round. A good beginning hike is the short, self-guided nature trail that introduces you to the native plants of the area.

Take the CA-12 exit off US 101 in Santa Rosa and continue on CA-12 to Farmers Lane. The freeway ends here, but continue across Farmers Lane. This becomes Hoen Avenue. Continue on Hoen until you reach Summerfield Road. Cross Summerfield, where Hoen becomes Newanga. Go straight to the park entrance. Continue past the base of the dam to the parking lot.

From the parking lot, walk down the paved road toward the swimming area; the nature trail is on the right. Read the map and plant guide at the head of the trail and then take the short walk to the south end of the trail. From there you can return to the parking lot and picnic area, or take another trail in the park.

The nature trail at Spring Lake features this spring-fed waterfall.

The trail around Spring Lake leads past many fine fishing holes.

76. Lake Trail Loop

Type:	Dayhike
Difficulty:	Moderate for children
Distance:	2.5 miles, loop
Hiking time:	1.5 hours
Elevation gain:	Minimal
Hikable:	Year-round
Map:	USGS Santa Rosa Topographic

Spring Lake is an artificial lake set among the oak and open grassland of the rolling hills to the east of Santa Rosa. The lake is regularly stocked with trout, and bass and blue gill that are easily caught by youngsters and oldsters alike. Fishing is far from the only attraction of the lake and the surrounding park, however; the swimming lagoon on the east side of the lake is popular with families during hot summers. The trails around the lake also offer a variety of hikes that can be enjoyed by the whole family. While many are paved with asphalt and are accessible year-round, even during the rainy season, others are dirt trails that take you to sections of the lake bank that feel isolated even if they aren't.

Follow the directions for hike 75, Nature Trail.

From the parking lot, cross the road and Spring Creek overflow channel to the dirt trail that heads northeast toward the lake. At the first fork take a right (the left takes you to the swimming lagoon), and another right at the second fork. This trail takes you into the edge of an oak forest uphill from the lake. Stay on the narrow footpath that parallels a wider path frequently used by horseback riders and bicyclists.

At about 0.25 mile, the trail begins a series of short ups and downs as it passes through underbrush of poison oak, toyon, and berries. The trees here are mostly oak with some madrone and buckeye, both of which have showy flower blooms during the spring. The buckeye are related to the chestnut, and they have large, hard brown seed pods in the late summer and fall.

The next junction is with a trail that leads downhill toward the lake, but stay on the upper trail, which offers views of the lake and lagoon. As you come to the next junction, take a left (the right fork goes to the Shady Oak Picnic Area) and cross the paved road. Turn north toward the dam.

The vegetation here includes tall stands of fennel, thickets of berry vines, and dense coyote brush. The trail passes a solitary cottonwood at about 0.5 mile and joins a paved path that leads across an inlet of the lake. After crossing the inlet the trail again becomes dirt, and follows along the shore through cottonwood, alder, and willow. The paved path runs across the top of the dam above, but it is more interesting to stay on the lower dirt path if it is not too wet. The shoreline is covered with tules, horsetail ferns, and other water plants that are home to many small birds and water animals.

At about 1 mile, near the end of the dam, the trail forks. Stay to the left along the shore of the lake. About 200 yards past the end of the dam a faint trail leads off to the right and heads toward Lake Ralphine in Howarth Park. Go straight along the shore of the lake and head toward the end of the West Dam of Spring Lake, which is reached at 1.25 miles into the hike.

The trail becomes gravel at the end of the dam and soon veers right past several large water tanks. Follow the horse trail signs and turn away from the tanks. As you pass a cinder block building, the trail becomes somewhat unclear, but veer to your right on the gravel road for another 100 yards to more horse trail signs. The trail follows beside a chain link fence for a while before turning back into oaks where there are plenty of wildflowers during the spring.

Near 1.75 miles the trail crosses a paved road, heads through a rocky area, and merges with another trail near the Jackrabbit Picnic Area. Continue east parallel to the paved road past the boat ramp.

At 2 miles near the Group Camping Area the path forks. Take the trail to the left across the dam to reach the parking area.

77. Rough Go/Spring Creek Trail Loop

Type: Dayhike
Difficulty: Difficult for children
Distance: 4.5 miles, loop
Hiking time: 3 hours
Elevation gain: 700 feet
Hikable: Year-round
Map: USGS Santa Rosa Topographic

Dozens of trails that total over 40 miles cross the 5000 acres of Annadel Park. This state park was formed after Santa Rosa residents realized that residential developments were likely to encroach on the rolling hills that had been used for a number of years as a hiking and picnic site by the public even though it was privately owned. By 1971 Sonoma County residents had raised over a million dollars to match state and federal funding. Since then the park has become a favorite destination of hikers, horseback riders, and mountain bikers, all of whom use the trails for their individual purposes. Hikers can head for 26-acre Lake Ilsanjo for a picnic or swim, Ledson Marsh for birdwatching, or simply explore the woodlands and meadows on an afternoon outing.

Follow the directions for hike 75, Nature Trail, to Spring Lake. Join Spring Creek Trail to the south of the horse trailer parking area.

Spring Creek Trail is a broad gravel trail that parallels channelized Spring Creek across a grassy meadow. Keep to the left at the first junction and cross a bridge at about 0.5 mile. Rough Go Trail heads to the left just past the bridge. The trail climbs steadily through scattered groves of coast live oak and black oaks. The grassland here is full of color during the spring as vetch, lupine, buttercups, and poppies all bloom.

Keep to the marked trails, although there are several unmarked spurs that lead off on both sides of the trail. Rough Go Trail makes sharp turns to the left and right as it continues its steady climb, passing some large boulders at 1 mile. This is a good place to take a rest and explore.

The trail continues to climb steadily, and just beyond the boulders, there is a panoramic vista of Spring Creek Canyon. In the next 0.5 mile, you pass two trails coming in from the left and reach the crest of the hill at the second one.

From 1.5 miles to just under 2 miles, Rough Go is relatively level and offers views of Mount St. Helena to the northeast and False Lake Meadow, where wildflowers add colorful blooms during the spring.

Just before the 2-mile mark there is a trail junction with six trails heading off in various directions. Three of these are unmarked. Continue on Rough Go, which is marked, and climb south above a large meadow, over which you can see Hood Mountain.

The trail begins to descend just after 2 miles, heading toward Lake Ilsanjo. Soon the trail takes a sharp left turn and the lake is right in front of you.

There are picnic tables and toilets, but no water, beside the dam. You can lunch or rest while overlooking the lake, which generally has plenty of waterfowl feeding in the tules around the shore.

The Spring Creek Trail joins Rough Go Trail just before the dam. Take a left at the junction and head back toward the trailhead. This trail has much more shade than Rough Go and is a pleasure on warm days when the afternoon sun can be enervating on the more exposed trails. During the spring, shade-loving wildflowers are found under the oak canopy, and ferns grow along the creek.

The trail makes a gradual descent, and an occasional vista to the north and west is available through openings in the forest. At places where the trail comes closer to the creek, let the children explore the creekside during a rest stop.

At about 3.75 miles (1.75 from the lake), Canyon Trail enters from the left, and at about 4 miles Spring Creek Trail joins Rough Go. From there return to the parking area.

Children are often still active when the adults must take a breather.

78. Lower Steve's S/W. P. Richardson Trail Loop

Type: Dayhike
Difficulty: Difficult for children
Distance: 4 miles, loop
Hiking time: 2 hours
Elevation gain: 500 feet
Hikable: Year-round
Map: USGS Santa Rosa Topographic

The 5000 acres of Annadel encompass a wide range of plant communities, including oak woodland with bay and madrone, fir and redwood forest, open grassland, and lake and marsh. This trail, like hike 77, takes you through several of these and has Lake Ilsanjo as a midpoint. This loop takes you through thick forests of Douglas fir and oak on the upward journey before crossing an open grassland just prior to reaching the lake. Broken pieces of obsidian are abundant along the trail, just as they were when the Southern Pomo Indians collected them for making arrowheads and spear points. Park rules prohibit *collection* of these today, but kids will still enjoy *searching* for them. The first leg of the hike is quite steep, but the return trip takes you down a more gentle slope.

Take the CA-12 exit off US 101 in Santa Rosa and head east. Continue across Farmers Lane at the end of the freeway. The street on the other side of Farmers Lane is Hoen Avenue. Continue on Hoen to Summerfield Road. Take a left on Summerfield and continue to the end, past Howarth Park. Turn right on Montgomery Drive and continue for a little over 1 mile to Channel Drive. Turn right on Channel Drive and go for just over 2 miles to the park entrance. The trail begins on the right side of the parking lot.

Take the W. P. Richardson Trail out of the parking lot. This is a broad gravel road that climbs gently to the southeast. After about 500 feet, take the Lower Steve's S Trail, which leads off to the right. This is a narrower, steeper trail than the Richardson Trail, but is much less crowded and is a more direct route to Lake Ilsanjo. It passes through a fir forest with the occasional bay tree, along with hedge nettle and poison oak, both plants that should be be avoided.

After less than 0.25 mile, many flakes of obsidian begin to show up along the dirt trail. While these are interesting to study while discussing with your children how the Native Americans used them to make projectile points, please do not collect them. Park rules prohibit the collec-

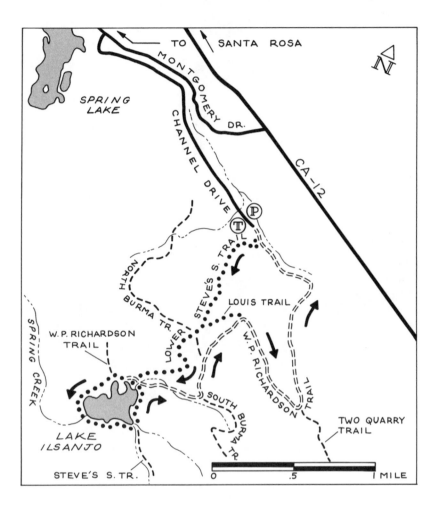

tion of any rocks or plants within park boundaries. The trail soon takes several sharp turns as it climbs steadily up the hillside. Many types of ferns (sword, bracken, maidenhair, and wood) can be seen along this section, as well as snowberry, false Solomon's seal, miner's lettuce, and wood rose.

The trail reaches a ridge with a heavy growth of large fir at about 0.5 mile; it levels off shortly thereafter. The forest becomes more mixed, with oak and bay becoming more numerous. After winding through this mixed forest, the trail again begins to climb until it connects with the Louis Trail at 0.75 mile. Stay to your right on Steve's S Trail; the trail crosses an open meadow that is covered with multi-hued flowers during the spring.

Broad, all-weather trails are used year-round in Sonoma County.

The trail soon meets the North Burma Trail from the right. At that junction, continue straight on Steve's S Trail but veer to the right at the junction immediately ahead. This is still Steve's S Trail, and it begins to drop in to the lake basin at 1 mile. Mount Bennett rises before you as you begin to cross the large meadow on the north shore of the lake. Chaparral, with lots of manzanita, grows along this section of the trail. Blue and yellow wildflowers predominate the profuse bloom here in the spring.

At just under 1.5 miles, the W. P. Richardson Trail crosses Lower Steve's S Trail. About 0.25 mile farther, you begin to skirt the east end of the lake and two trail spurs lead to picnic tables and toilets. This is an excellent spot to spend a leisurely lunch and explore the lakeshore, where there are many small water animals and birds living among the rushes and cattails.

To return to the trailhead, go back to the junction of the Lower Steve's S and W. P. Richardson trails and turn right onto the W. P. Richardson Trail. The first short section of the trail ascends to the ridge above Lake Ilsanjo and soon joins the South Burma Trail, which leads right to Ledson Marsh. Continue on the W. P. Richardson Trail by turning left at this junction. For the next 0.25 mile the trail leads through a large meadow with scattered oaks. From there the trail descends more rapidly and enters a fir and oak forest.

As the trail passes the junction with the Louis Trail on the left at 2 miles, it takes a sharp right turn and levels off. On the right of the trail there are large outcroppings of basalt and the remains of an old quarry. You can explore these as you take a rest stop.

The trail continues to descend gradually, and the forest now includes some redwoods with the fir and oak. you pass the junction with the Two Quarry Trail at 3 miles from the trailhead. Take the W. P. Richardson Trail to the left. The rest of the trail offers good views of the hills to the north.

79. Ledson Marsh Trail

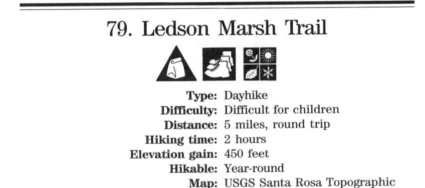

Type: Dayhike
Difficulty: Difficult for children
Distance: 5 miles, round trip
Hiking time: 2 hours
Elevation gain: 450 feet
Hikable: Year-round
Map: USGS Santa Rosa Topographic

Large tracts of wild, or at least fairly wild, land abound within Annadel State Park, tracts where few hikers venture, and where wild pigs and deer are found in abundance. One such site is Ledson Marsh in the eastern part of the park, far from the Santa Rosa trailheads. There are two trailheads, Lawndale and Schulz, off CA-12 near Oakmont that are secluded and lightly used. These both lead into the area around Ledson Marsh where dozens of species of birds can be seen, as well as wild pigs, which are populous enough to be considered pests that destroy native plants and the habitats of native wildlife.

Take the CA-12 exit off US 101 in Santa Rosa. Continue east to the end of the freeway and turn left on Farmers Lane. This is now CA-12.

Go past Montgomery Village to Fourth Street. Turn right. This is now CA-12 again. Continue for about 7 miles east to Lawndale Road. Turn right and go just over 1 mile to Lawndale Trailhead. Ledson Marsh is a 4-mile round trip from here, but the hike described here begins at the Schulz Trailhead. Continue past the Lawndale Trailhead for another 0.5 mile to Schulz Road, turn right, and in just less than 1 mile there is a small parking lot at the Schulz Trailhead.

Schulz Trail climbs gently through a mixed forest of Douglas fir, oak, and madrone, with a thick undercover that includes some chaparral such as manzanita and coyote brush. After a short distance the trail breaks out of this dense forest and begins to descend slowly through a thick cover of Scotch broom, whose yellow flowers are dominant in the spring.

The trail follows the edge of Schulz Canyon, which is lined with large fir, big-leaf maple, and bay. Many blue flowers are found underneath during the spring. Just past 0.25 mile, the trail crosses a seasonal creek whose banks are covered with thick tangles of wild grape, berries, and poison oak. As the trail begins to climb along the creek there is a stand of redwood on the right.

The trail begins to turn right at about 0.5 mile and then climbs through open grassland that has some scattered black and coast live oak, as well as some patches of manzanita. The trail continues to climb, and soon Sonoma Mountain is visible to the south and Bald and Red mountains to the north in Sugar Loaf Ridge State Park.

The climb eases at 1 mile where an old stone wall that was built

The trail into Ledson Marsh is filled with many an obstacle.

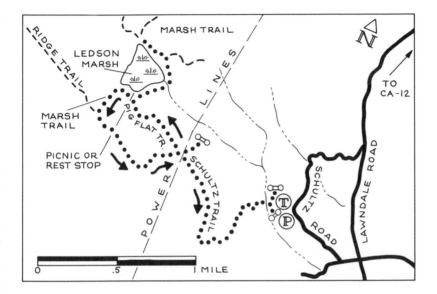

in the 1800s now marks part of the park boundary. The trail again begins to climb as it heads toward some large power lines and turns away from the stone wall. At about 1.25 miles, the trail heads through an area of thick chaparral as it climbs to the top of a rocky hill. After 1.5 miles the trail drops again and reenters a forest and meets a broader trail, Pig Flat Trail. Go right. After less than 100 feet Pig Flat Trail enters a meadow and joins with two other trails. On the left is the Ridge Trail; on the right a deadend spur. Continue straight ahead on the Pig Flat Trail, which again climbs into a fir forest. Just under 2 miles it again drops into a meadow and then resumes its upward climb. It levels off around 2 miles and begins the descent to Ledson Marsh.

The trail ends at Ledson Marsh at just over 2 miles. Picnic tables at the junction are placed to allow you to look at the marsh and its many birds during a break for exploring.

Ducks, grebes, mudhens, and other waterfowl are often seen here, and quail can be seen and heard in the surrounding grassland. A broad trail encircles the marsh and offers closeup views of many of the birds.

After exploring and resting, head southwest on the Marsh Trail, which circles the west side of the marsh, past the junction with Pig Flat Trail, and uphill away from Ledson Marsh to climb through a forest. Marsh Trail joins Ridge Trail, which runs along the park boundary, at just under 2.5 miles. Turn left here on Ridge Trail and follow the old rock wall back down the hill until Ridge Trail rejoins Schulz Trail at about 4 miles. Turn right on Schulz Trail and continue back to the trailhead.

80. Santa Rosa Creek Trail

Type:	Dayhike
Difficulty:	Difficult for children
Distance:	3.5 miles, round trip
Hiking time:	2 hours
Elevation gain:	650 feet
Hikable:	Year-round
Map:	USGS Kenwood Topographic

The headwaters of Santa Rosa Creek are found among the steep canyons to the east of the city in Hood mountain Regional Park. This park is open only on weekends, and is generally closed during the peak fire season during the summer and early fall because of the extreme fire danger that exists on the dry canyon slopes. Hikes in this area take you into desolate wilderness that appears untouched by humans, although suburbia lies less than 5 miles away along Los Alamos Road.

Take the CA-12 exit off US 101 in Santa Rosa, and follow the CA-12 signs for just over 6 miles to the east, toward Sonoma. Turn left on Los Alamos Road and continue for just under 5 miles past several sub-divisions up the steep, winding road to the parking lot at Hood Mountain Regional Park.

A gravel road leads to the left out of the parking lot into steep grass-covered hillsides dotted with oak. After about 200 yards, the road turns into a dirt trail and begins to drop rapidly. Coyote bush covers the hills beside the trail until you reach the site of an old homestead at about 0.25 mile. After the homestead you will pass scattered madrone, bay, oak, and Douglas fir before the forest becomes dense with different species of oak.

At 0.5 mile, the trail takes a sharp turn to the right and descends even more rapidly. You enter the park here, and can see several canyons that contain the headwaters of different forks of Santa Rosa Creek. A trail branches off to the right just before you reach the old parking lot of the park. There are several picnic tables here, and you may want to stop here on the way back to the parking lot. For now, take the next trail to the right and continue past a water faucet and horse trough as the trail makes a sweeping S. More picnic tables overlook a grass-covered slope that leads down to the headwaters of Santa Rosa Creek.

At 0.75 mile a trail leads off to the left toward the Alder Glen Picnic Area. The main trail continues downhill along the creek. You cross a tributary and climb and descend again before climbing to where it joins

Moss-covered boulders are fun to play on during dry times.

the creek at about 1 mile. The trail levels and then climbs and drops gently as it follows the contours of the canyon. California buckeye grow along this section of the trail.

Homestead Meadows await you just beyond 1 mile, and the trail makes a gradual descent for another 0.25 mile, joining a broad road where the remains of a small shed stand beside a rock outcropping. Take a left around the rock and you come to Santa Rosa Creek. The creek banks are overgrown with alder and bay. A trail fords the creek and heads to the top of Hood Mountain (another 4 miles), but take the trail to the right just before the ford. This follows the creek to the west. A dense growth of Woodwardia ferns cover the opposite banks of the creek along this section of the trail.

At just over 1.5 miles, the trail veers to the left and drops as you cross a footbridge across a tributary to Santa Rosa Creek. The trail narrows to a path and leads along a rock outcropping that is covered with hanging

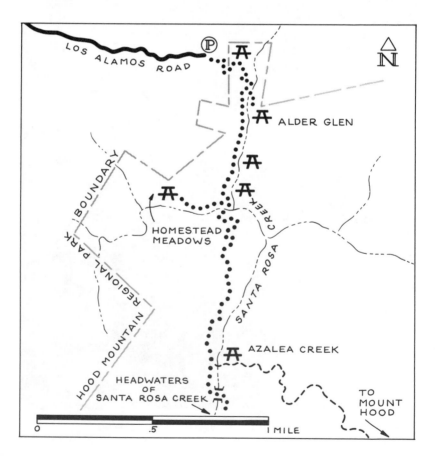

ferns. The trail ends at 1.75 miles at the creek headwaters. From here the creek drops more than 400 feet on its way toward Santa Rosa, where it has been channelized as it passes through developed areas.

From here backtrack up the trail to the parking lot.

---

81. Creekside Nature Trail

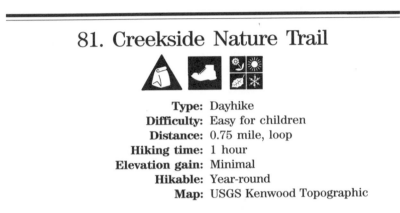

Type:	Dayhike
Difficulty:	Easy for children
Distance:	0.75 mile, loop
Hiking time:	1 hour
Elevation gain:	Minimal
Hikable:	Year-round
Map:	USGS Kenwood Topographic

Sugarloaf Ridge State Park is a 2700-acre park nestled in the Mayacamas Range about a 0.5-hour drive east of Santa Rosa. More than 25 miles of trails lead through the park, and some take you to the top of peaks that reach more than 2700 feet above sea level. This short trail

A sprawling madrone makes a good resting place for a tired hiker.

is a good one to take as an introduction to the flora and fauna of the park, and as a way to avoid the searing heat of the summer. Although Native Americans lived in the area for hundreds of years before the first Europeans settled in California, little of the land in the park was used after the Wappo village of the Wilikos was wiped out by a cholera epidemic in 1833 and a smallpox epidemic in 1838. Most of the survivors of these two epidemics were relocated to a reservation in what is now Mendocino County.

Take the CA-12 exit off US 101 in Santa Rosa and follow the signs east toward Sonoma for 11 miles to Adobe Canyon Road. Turn left on Adobe Canyon and continue about 2.5 miles up the steep, winding road

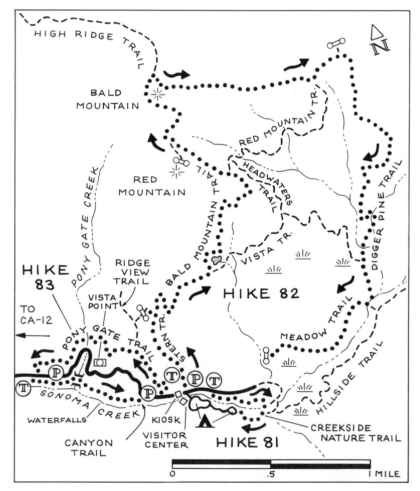

to the park entrance. Park in the first lot past the visitor center and cross the road to the beginning of the Creekside Nature Trail. A stop at the visitor center with its exhibits on the park is a good idea before taking the hike.

This 0.75-mile hike, which was built by the Youth Conservation Corps, leads along the banks of Sonoma Creek and numbered posts correspond to descriptions on the back page of the park brochure and hiking map available at the visitor center. Many plants found in the park are located along the trail, and with a little luck you may see some of the animals and birds that are residents of the area.

Near the midway point of the trail, a short spur leads to a bench where you can sit and enjoy the quiet solitude offered by the forest.

The last half of the trail offers vistas of the surrounding peaks as well as samples of local plants.

82. Stern Trail

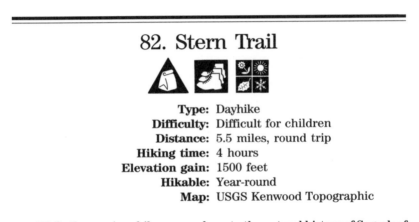

Type: Dayhike
Difficulty: Difficult for children
Distance: 5.5 miles, round trip
Hiking time: 4 hours
Elevation gain: 1500 feet
Hikable: Year-round
Map: USGS Kenwood Topographic

While the previous hike exposed you to the natural history of Sugarloaf Ridge State Park, this one takes you to the top of the highest peak in the park. From there you will have views of all of Sonoma County, from the vineyards of Kenwood and the Sonoma Valley and Mount St. Helena to the north and east to the Santa Rosa Plains to the west. Two of the three distinct ecological systems found in the park are crossed by the trail to the top of Bald Mountain. Chaparral-covered ridges and oak and fir woodlands with open meadows are both represented. Only the redwood forests of Sonoma Creek Canyon are missing. Since summers can be hot and dry in the park, and only occasionally moderated by ocean fog, this hike is most enjoyable in the spring and fall.

Follow directions for hike 81, Creekside Nature Trail, to reach Sugarloaf Ridge State Park. Once inside the park, continue past the visitor center and park in the lot on the left uphill from the center. Restrooms and picnic facilities are across the road from the parking lot. The Stern Trail begins about 100 yards downhill.

This trail, which is well marked with the blue map sign of the Bay Area Ridge Trail, was dedicated to philanthropist Marjorie Stern, who donated what was once a private road to her hilltop ranch—and 320 acres—to the park to help with the development of the Bay Area Ridge Trail. It became a link in the Bay Area Ridge Trail and connects with the Bald Mountain Trail. Bald Mountain, at 2729 feet, is the tallest peak in Sugarloaf Ridge State Park and the second highest peak in Sonoma County.

The trail swings around the base of Red Mountain as it winds uphill past a marshy area. It continues to climb gently and reaches a junction with the Bald Mountain Trail at about 0.5 mile. The gate to Stern Ranch is on the left, but the trail continues on the other side of the vehicle barrier. Bald Mountain Trail is paved here and moves in and out of chaparral and oak woodlands. The various wildflowers in nature's display include the rare yellow fairy lantern, a miniature lily. This is one of the few trails in the Bay Area where it can be seen. See if your children can find these elusive flowers with the enchanting name.

There are several benches along this stretch of trail that offer views of Sugarloaf Ridge and a chance to rest. The trail passes by some vineyards, and Little Bald Mountain comes into view before the junction of Bald Mountain and Vista trails at just under 1 mile. This is a good turnaround for youngsters who might not think they can make it up the mountain. Vista Trail takes you back to the parking area via the Digger Pine and Meadow trails. To continue to Bald Mountain, stay left.

For the next 0.5 mile the trail continues its upward climb, passing a small vernal pool area that is filled with wildflowers after the last rains. It goes through chaparral where the manzanita are as big as madrone trees. There is also a poison oak plant as big as a tree that is estimated to be several hundred years old. Another bench is located just past the chaparral area and offers a view over the top of scrub oaks.

At about 1.75 miles the Red Mountain Trail heads off to the right; it offers another loop back to the parking lot for those who are tired. Several hundred yards farther along the trail is the only picnic table along the trail to the top of Bald Mountain. This is a good place to stop for an energy break before the climb to the peak.

The vegetation along this section of the trail includes madrone, oak, and big-leaf maple. In fact, the largest big-leaf maple in California is found in this grove.

The trail to the microwave station atop Red Mountain takes off to the left at about 2 miles, and the dirt road to the right continues on to Bald Mountain. This road curves around the mountain where both sides are lined with poppies during the spring bloom. Explain to your children that the microwave station on Red Mountain is not a large oven for

Not everone is always happy on the trail.

cooking snacks, but is a relay station for transmitting telephone, TV, and radio messages. One story has it that the use of microwaves to cook food was discovered at a relay station such as this one when someone's lunch was left on the edge of the microwave transmitter and the owner found it cooked by the microwaves!

The Bald Mountain Trail ends at the next junction, at a little over 2 miles. To the left is the High Ridge Trail. To the right is the Digger Pine Trail (which is being renamed the Gray Pine Trail at the request of Native Americans). Take this and then the first right to complete your climb to the peak.

Return to the parking lot by backtracking, or head down the Digger Pine Trail, which adds 1 more mile to the hike, for a change of scenery.

83. Sonoma Canyon/Pony Gate Loop

Type: Dayhike
Difficulty: Moderate for children
Distance: 1.75 miles, loop
Hiking time: 1 hour
Elevation gain: 560 feet
Hikable: Year-round
Map: USGS Kenwood Topographic

Although Sugarloaf Ridge State Park is generally considered a hot, dry park, this image is quickly dispelled when this trail is taken in early spring. The winter rains and subsequent runoff fill the creek to overflowing, and the waterfall roars as the water tumbles down the canyon. The rains also give life to the bright colors of spring wildflowers that cover the hillsides in sharp contrast to the light green foliage that is emerging from the deciduous trees that line the banks of the creek.

Follow directions for hike 81, Creekside Nature Trail, and continue into the park several hundred yards. Watch carefully for a wide turnout about 100 yards past the Canyon Trail trailhead.

The trail begins with a descent through a redwood and fir forest until it is about 50 feet above Sonoma Creek. The undergrowth here is thick and lush with a mixture of wildflowers, native grasses, and other riparian growth.

The trail continues to descend as it passes alongside the fern-covered creek bank. After about 200 yards, the trail crosses Pony Gate Creek where it joins Sonoma Creek by means of a bridge. The bridge is a good overlook for viewing the creeks as they rush down the steep canyon below. To the left Sugarloaf Ridge can be seen a mile away and 1200 feet higher.

The trail continues upstream, and in just under 0.25 mile you can get your first glimpse of the waterfall above some rapids. Black oaks, bay, alder, and sycamore grow along this section of the creek.

Soon after the first sighting of the waterfall the trail climbs some steps up through moss- and fern-covered rocks beside the falls, but before the steps, take a short spur that leads to the right to the base of the falls. When they are running full, the falls send a spray of mist over the surrounding vegetation and anyone standing near the falls.

Return to the main trail, which climbs up the side of the rocky canyon and passes through thick stands of ferns. After a steady, steep climb to the top of the falls, the trail levels out somewhat and then broadens just before 0.5 mile. It makes a left turn and continues to climb between large boulders in an oak forest.

The trail soon turns away from the creek and levels for a while before beginning a gentle climb. At 0.5 mile, the trail crosses a seasonal creek with a small clearing, bends to the right, and climbs out of the thick forest canopy. Toyon and other bush-like plants thrive here. The trail crosses another small creek and turns to the left to follow the creek upstream.

At about 0.75 mile, the trail crosses a paved road near the entrance kiosk to become Pony Gate Trail on the other side. Pony Gate climbs into open grassland and then winds into a hardwood forest. As the trail bends sharply to the left it stays in the forest but skirts a large open glade. Deer and other wildlife can often be seen here.

The trail follows the contour of the steep hillside, climbs through a small clearing that overlooks Sonoma Creek Canyon, and passes between two old and misshapened oaks. A trail comes in from the right, but stay to the left under the oaks. The Pony Gate Trail crosses over a dry and rocky creek bed (it generally has water immediately after a heavy rain, but soon dries up), turns left, and crosses another small creek before the Ridge View Trail joins it from the right at 1 mile.

The Pony Gate Trail begins to descend here. Be careful—the clay soil of the trail can be slippery after a rain. The trail continues steadily downward through an oak woodland and across open meadows until just past 1.25 miles when it descends into a dark forest. It then crosses a rocky canyon and drops steeply to Pony Gate Creek. At just under 1.5 miles, it crosses Pony Gate Creek and climbs steeply for about 100 feet. It levels out somewhat and soon joins an old road, which then heads back downhill.

You can see the road below (at 1.75 miles) as the trail descends through a mixed hardwood forest. Your parking space is just uphill from where the trail joins the road.

The Wolf House ruins are fascinating to the whole family.

84. Wolf House Ruins Trail

Type:	Dayhike
Difficulty:	Moderate for children
Distance:	1.5 miles, round trip
Hiking time:	1 hour
Elevation gain:	200 feet
Hikable:	Year-round
Map:	USGS Glen Ellen Topographic

Jack London was one of the most famous authors of the early twentieth century, and he moved to Beauty Ranch in Glen Ellen in 1905 when he purchased the first 127 acres. Between then and 1913 he continued to expand his holdings, and began to build the home of his dreams, Wolf House. Unfortunately, the house burned just before London and his wife were to move in. London was said to never recover from this devastating loss, and the ruins stand today as they were left in 1913.

Take the CA-12 exit off US 101 in Santa Rosa and continue on CA-12 for 12 miles east of Santa Rosa. Turn left on Arnold Drive and go for not quite 1 mile to downtown Glen Ellen. As Arnold Drive takes a sharp turn to the left, London Ranch Road heads off to the right. Take this road for a little over 1 mile to the park entrance. The trail to Wolf House ruins heads south from the front of the House of Happy Walls, which was built by London's widow, Charmain, and now houses a small museum and the park visitor center.

The gravel trail leads past an exhibit of farm equipment that was used at Beauty Ranch, and then turns left as it descends through a mixed forest with buckeye, madrone, oak, bay, and some young fir. The trail levels out at about 0.25 mile and travels along the edge of a meadow

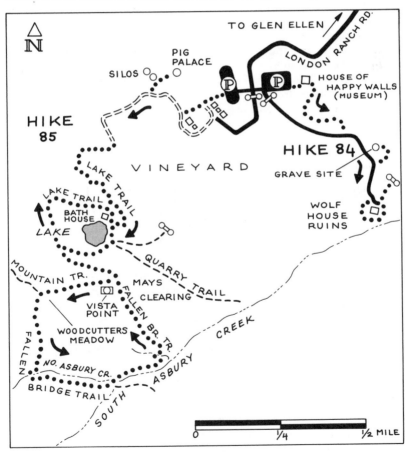

that is full of poppies, Indian paintbrush, and buttercups in the spring.

At the end of the meadow, the trail crosses a small creek and climbs for a short distance before it drops again and comes to another creek. There is a rest bench and drinking fountain here.

The trail crosses another creek and comes to a broad paved path at just under 0.5 mile. Shortly you'll come to a junction with another bench and drinking fountain. Veer to the right, where the trail drops gently as it leads along the edge of a grassy hillside with old fruit trees on the right. On the left is a stand of live and black oaks.

The trail drops more abruptly as you approach the Wolf House ruins at 0.75 mile. The ruins are surrounded by a grove of redwood trees and stand high above the banks of Asbury Creek. Have your children read *The Call of the Wild?* If so, have them guess why London called his house "Wolf House."

A trail leads you around the ruins, and there are some benches and a drinking fountain near the east side of the ruins.

As you retrace your steps back uphill, take a right at the first junction. This short spur trail takes you to London's grave site, where a large red lava marker stands.

Return to the main trail and continue to the junction with the dirt trail you descended from the House of Happy Walls. Here you may return the way you came or continue up the paved path to the parking lot.

85. Lake/Fallen Bridge Trail Loop

Type: Dayhike
Difficulty: Difficult for children
Distance: 4.5 miles, round trip
Hiking time: 2 hours
Elevation gain: 800 feet
Hikable: Year-round
Map: USGS Glen Ellen Topographic

Jack London bought some of the most beautiful and wild land in Sonoma County to enlarge his ranch, Beauty Ranch. The forests that cover the slopes of Sonoma Mountain still maintain that feeling of wildness, and the trails lead through stands of fir and redwood, interlaced with an occasional glade filled with wildflowers, seemingly far from civilization. Fallen tree trunks are covered with moss; wild grape and honey-

The rushes at water's edge are fun to explore.

suckle wind around standing trees; and ferns cover creek banks after the winter rains. Even the lake that London created seems almost to blend in with the surrounding forests.

Follow the directions for hike 84, Wolf House Ruins Trail, but turn to the right after the park entrance to enter the upper parking lot. Pass through the grove of eucalyptus that London planted to the beginning of Lake Trail.

The trail passes by the farm buildings that London built to house his horses and pigs and the stone distillery building before a short spur leads off to the left to the cottage and barns. You can take a look at London's cottage and the outbuildings by taking the side trails off to the left and then returning to the main trail afterward.

The main trail turns sharply to the right where the spur leads off to the left to the cottage, and forks again after about 100 yards. Take a right at this fork, which takes you past a vineyard on your left. The road soon takes a sharp turn to the left, and a trail leads off to the right. This spur leads to the Pig Palace and some old silos. Take the road to the left as it winds around the vineyard.

The trail continues a gentle climb until just before 0.5 mile, where it leaves the vineyard and leads into the forest. There is a gate on the road there, and a trail branches off to the right. While equestrians and mountain bikers must continue on the road, hikers will find the trail a more pleasant ascent to the lake.

The trail leads through a mixed forest with plenty of large fir and redwood towering over the understory of bay, big-leaf maple, and madrone. At 0.75 mile, the trail forks again. Take the less traveled trail to the right and continue climbing to the next fork, which is at 1 mile. This fork leads you to the lake, bathhouse, and dam. There is a nice beach here where you can rest and wade along the shore among cattails and rushes. You may wish to make this stop on your return trip, however.

Take the road across the dam at the east end of the 5-acre lake and continue uphill on the road past the Quarry Trail, which takes off to the right. At about 1.5 miles, the Lake Trail joins the road from the right. (This is the trail you will take on your return trip.)

The road continues through a mixed forest of fir, madrone, bay, and oak and enters Mays Clearing at just under 1.75 miles. The view here is of the slopes of Sonoma Mountain to the southeast and the north end of San Francisco Bay down the Valley of the Moon. Several trails also join here; Fallen Bridge Trail leads off to the left and the Mountain Trail to the right.

Take the Mountain Trail upward as it climbs back into the forest and along the north slope of a ridge. Near 2 miles the upper end of Fallen Bridge Trail joins the Mountain Trail at Woodcutter's Meadow. Take this trail as it crosses a saddle of the ridge and climbs to cross North Asbury Creek at 2.25 miles before descending steeply down the slope. Fallen Bridge Trail follows the creek to about 2.5 miles where the trail splits. The trail that continues straight ahead crosses South Asbury Creek and heads onto Sonoma State Hospital land. Veer to the left and cross back over North Asbury Creek as the trail continues to descend.

At less than 2.75 miles, the trail takes a sharp turn away from North Asbury creek, crosses a tributary, and climbs for a short distance before entering Mays Clearing from the southeast. The vista point here is a good place to take a short rest stop.

Fallen Bridge Trail ends at Mountain Trail just past Mays Clearing. Descend Mountain Trail to the sharp right turn just past 3 miles. The Lake Trail heads off to the left in the middle of the sharp turn and takes you around the north side of the lake. This may be the best time to take a break at the lake and bathhouse because the major portion of the hike is over.

From the lake, retrace your route back to the parking lot.

86. Canyon/Ridge Trail Loop

Type: Dayhike
Difficulty: Moderate for children
Distance: 2.5 miles, loop
Hiking time: 2 hours
Elevation gain: 300 feet
Hikable: Year-round
Map: USGS Glen Ellen

For many years Sonoma State Hospital used the 162 acres of rolling hills now included in the Sonoma Valley Regional Park as a dairy. Sonoma County acquired the land in 1973 and as of 1991 was busy developing a comprehensive trail system that crisscrosses the ridges and canyons in the park. The slopes of the canyons are studded with oak, and wildflowers add color during the spring before the grass turns golden. The ridges offer expansive views of Glen Ellen, the Valley of the Moon, and the mountain ranges to the west and north.

Take the CA-12 exit off US 101 in Santa Rosa and continue on CA-12 for 12.5 miles east of Santa Rosa. Turn right into Sonoma Valley Regional Park.

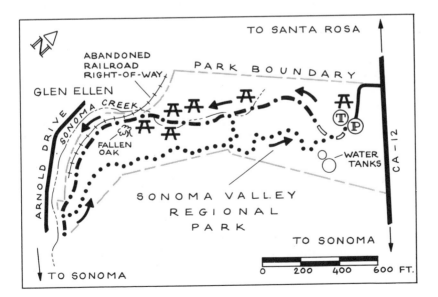

The small wonders of nature are seen when eyes are kept to the ground.

The trail heads out of the parking lot toward two large green water tanks as a paved path. It turns right after about 100 yards and begins a gentle drop through open grassland that is full of poppies in the spring. A seasonal creek begins at a spring located by a picnic area, and it and the trail cross each other a number of times.

At about 0.25 mile, the creek crosses to the left of the trail near steep slopes, but the trail continues to descend. Soon the creek recrosses the trail and there are more picnic tables beside the creek.

At 0.5 mile, a dirt trail climbs up the side of the canyon to the left; however, you should stay on the paved path as it crosses the creek again. This area is full of wildflowers as early as January, when white milkmaids bloom in abundance.

Sonoma Mountain appears in the west as the trail continues to drop, and it soon passes another picnic table near an oak draped with poison oak vines. An old Oregon oak and buckeye, bay, and live oaks are all found nearby.

The trail passes a small canyon on the left and begins to climb to a small rise as the creek moves away to the right. At 0.75 mile, there is an old fallen oak and several picnic tables just before the old railroad right-of-way. The paved trail veers left and curves back to the right before it joins the right-of-way.

A grove of madrone surrounds the trail along this section as Sonoma Creek runs along the south side of the trail. At 1 mile, a dirt trail runs parallel between the paved one and the creek and a large manzanita bush and dozens of soap plants thrive nearby.

At about 1.25 miles, the trail divides into three forks. A dirt trail leads up the hill to the left, the gravel railbed veers to the left in the center, and the paved trail turns sharply to the right. The latter climbs a small hill to more picnic tables and soon comes to a gate near Arnold Drive. Those who want to take the easiest way back should simply return on the paved path. Others should take the dirt path to the left as it climbs around the end of a fence and heads northward. Large boulders lie beside the trail along this section, and wildflowers bloom beneath the scattered oak trees.

Just short of 1.75 miles, the trail takes a sharp right and begins a steep climb. At the top of the ridge the trail reaches the park boundary, bends left, and begins descending along the ridge. At the first fork the trail to the left drops abruptly back to the paved path. Continue to the right as the trail slowly descends along the fence line.

The trail soon climbs to the top of the ridge with views of the Valley of the Moon before dropping again until it becomes level at 2 miles. It climbs and drops again before coming to another fork. Stay to the right, passing views of the state hospital and Lake Suttonfield until you come to a maze of trails at 2.25 miles. Take the most used trail and continue downhill through a grove of small oak until the trail merges with an old road. Follow the well-traveled trail to the top of the last small ridge. From there the trail descends to the green water tanks and the parking lot.

87. Sonoma Creek Trail Loop

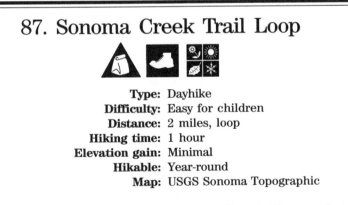

Type: Dayhike
Difficulty: Easy for children
Distance: 2 miles, loop
Hiking time: 1 hour
Elevation gain: Minimal
Hikable: Year-round
Map: USGS Sonoma Topographic

The Maxwell Farms Regional Park is small, only 85 acres, but it offers a pleasant short outing for residents of Sonoma even though it sits near one of the busiest intersections in the town. The park was once the farm of George Maxwell, a conservationist at the turn of the century who fought for the rights of small farmers. The park was later owned by a foundation named after him. In 1988 Sonoma County dedicated the area

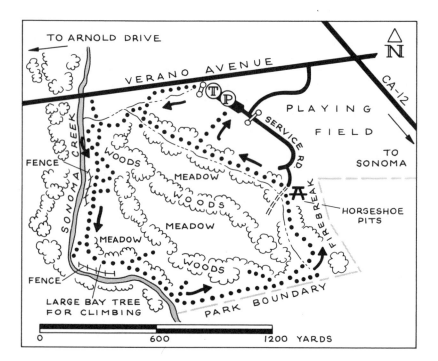

as a regional park, and its fields and woods have proved very popular to hikers and picnickers.

Take the US 101 exit in Santa Rosa and continue on CA-12 to the north edge of Sonoma. Turn right on Verano Avenue and take a quick left into the park.

The trail heads toward Sonoma Mountain out of the gravel overflow parking lot and crosses a creek at about 100 yards. Turn left after you cross the creek and continue parallel to Verano Avenue as the trail leads toward a stand of oak and then a stand of English walnuts. Berries and other low-growing bushes grow along the trail, along with some bay trees.

At 0.25 mile, the trail forks, and the broad path to the left is heavily used by mountain bikers. Continue straight as the trail drops near Sonoma Creek. It soon veers to the left, leaving the creek farther to the west. A spur trail heads through a jungle of vines, brambles, and small bushes along the creek as the main trail parallels the creek passing through wildflowers in the spring.

The trail soon climbs to meet the broad trail again, but immediately heads through a growth of poison oak on the right. A large bay tree, 8 feet in diameter and about 100 feet tall, stands to the right of the trail and a meadow is visible to the left.

At just under 0.5 mile, a fence prevents you from making a 20-foot drop to the creek below, and the trail veers to skirt the meadow. Soon you take the lower path to the right along the creek bank, where willows and cottonwoods form a thick barrier.

The trail soon returns to the meadow where it again forks. Continue straight into the woods. At just over 0.5 mile, another spur veers off to the right to drop about 150 feet to the creek, and the main trail continues straight before it turns to the left and returns to the meadow and fire break. About 100 feet past the turn there is another large bay tree near the trail that is an excellent climbing tree. Another fence runs along the high creek bank behind the bay to keep hikers from falling off the steep cliff. Just past the tree a path heads across the meadow toward the parking lot, and the main trail veers to the right along the fire break. Take the main trail to complete the loop, although you may take the trail to the left if you want to cut the hike short.

Around 0.75 mile, the trail turns left at the park boundary. It then heads east through open grassland. Continue past one fire road that leads off to the left to a second one about 50 yards farther along. Take the dirt trail that veers left into the woods at 0.75 mile and winds in and out of them until it reaches a horseshoe pit and picnic area just before 1 mile.

Cross the service road here and continue on the trail through a wild section of the park where wild grapevines hang from oak and bay. Several paths branch off in this area, but continue to the right as the trail crosses a meadow and climbs a small hill before returning to the parking lot.

Sprawling and fallen trees are great places to climb.

88. Tubb's Island Trail Loop

Type: Dayhike
Difficulty: Moderate for children
Distance: 7.5 miles, round trip
Hiking time: 3 hours
Elevation gain: Level
Hikable: Year-round
Map: USGS Sears Point Topographic

This trail in San Pablo Bay National Wildlife Refuge is different from most in this guide since it is level (nowhere in the entire refuge is higher than 20 feet above sea level) and almost treeless. The views are there, but they are eye-level ones of the northern reaches of San Pablo Bay and the farmland there that was reclaimed (a misnomer if there ever was one, for something must have been claimed once before it can be re-claimed) from the marshlands that are home to more than 200 species of birds and many small mammals, some of which are endangered species. The walk is pleasant, with few hikers to interfere with the solitude, but from mid-October to mid-January many pheasant hunters stalk the fields surrounding the trail.

Take the CA-37 exit off US 101 and continue 7.5 miles east to the intersection of CA-37 and CA-121. Park in the gravel parking area on the right just over the railroad tracks from the stoplight at the intersection. The trailhead is the gate to the east of the parking area.

The trail into the refuge is a dirt road that leads between fields on the left and open land on the right. Since this is land that was once part of the marsh, a canal is on one side of the road and Tolay Creek on the other.

The road takes several sharp turns in the first 0.5 mile as it winds through areas rich with large scrub and birds such as redwing blackbirds, quail, and pheasant. At 0.5 mile, a large eucalyptus looms on the left side of the road. This is the only shade on the entire hike and is also a roosting site for a variety of owls and hawks. Owl pellets in various stages of decomposition can be found underneath the tree. Owl pellets are the undigested remains of small rodents that the owl spits up. These small pellets are composed primarily of the fur and bones of the rodents, and by carefully tearing the pellet apart you can separate the bones from the fur. Complete skulls can often be found in the pellets, and these can sometimes be identified by looking in a field guide on rodents. Even if a definite identification cannot be made, children will be fascinated by this natural process.

Young hikers are also fascinated by the large number of shotgun

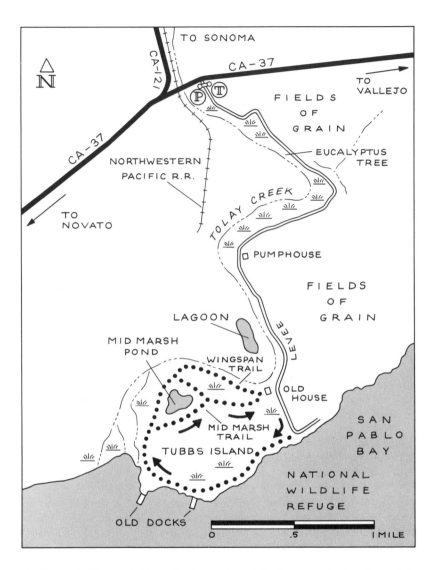

shells and rifle cartridges that can be picked up roadside along this stretch.

If the day is clear, and you happened to bring along a compass, look due south from the eucalyptus and you may be able to spot the Transamerica Building in downtown San Francisco.

Continue past the eucalyptus, and at two sharp bends near 0.75 mile two sloughs come together on your left. Pass the farm road that leads off to the left. After several right turns between 0.75 and 1 mile, the road gradually turns to the left before making a sharp turn to the left at 1.5 miles. Along this section, you can leave the road and walk on the levees on either side or head through some of the low-lying scrub to attempt to flush pheasant out of the underbrush.

After the sharp turn at 1.5 miles, the road again turns left and passes a metal pump house. The road has made a very slight elevation gain along this section, and on top of the levee near the pump house you can see the top of the towers of both the Richmond and Golden Gate bridges, as well as the top of some of the skyscrapers in downtown San Francisco. Mount Diablo can be seen to the southeast.

Coyote brush and other coastal scrub grow along both sides of the road here, and at 2 miles a lagoon appears on your right. As the road makes several turns, Angel Island, as well as other landmarks, can be seen to the south.

At 2.5 miles, there is a sign that states you are entering Lower Tubb's Island Wildlife Refuge. Dogs and hunting are prohibited beyond this point.

An old house leans against the wind beside a canal, and Wingspan Trail forks to the right as it heads toward the tidal flats. Continue straight. Another trail soon forks to the right. Continue on the main road to the open bay. There is farmland on the left and salt marsh on the right.

Around 3 miles, the road splits at the shore of the bay. At minus tide in the fall and winter, thousands of migrating birds feed here. Turn right and head south, with the bay to your left and the salt marsh to your right. The trail soon crosses a gate where the slough and marsh empty into the bay if the tide is going out.

The trail and levee wind left and right, and at about 3.5 miles, an old dock exists where ferries unloaded people and supplies for stagecoaches headed to Sonoma in the 1870s. Another gate is crossed and the ruins of another ferry dock are passed at 3.75 miles.

Continue on the levee, which turns northwest at Tolay Creek. At 4.25 miles, take the Mid Marsh Trail across the slough back toward the old house. Great and snowy egrets live and feed here along with an abundance of other birds.

The trail forks just past 4.5 miles. To the left a trail makes a loop to explore Mid Marsh Pond. Continue straight ahead to the big pond on the right at 4.75 miles that is surrounded by a large salt marsh. While this may look like lifeless land, it is one of the most productive habitats in the world. Each handful of muck from the bottom of these saltwater marshes contains millions of tiny organisms that are at the bottom of the food chain. These are eaten by larger organisms, which are, in turn, eaten by still larger ones. Waterfowl such as ducks and geese, and water birds such as herons, godwits, plovers, and egrets, and animals such as rodents and raccoons all feed and breed in this bountiful nursery.

For the next 0.25 mile, the trail can be swampy and brushy, but it soon regains high ground and merges with the outer loop path at just past 5 miles.

Retrace your path back 2.5 miles to the parking area.

The peaks and ridges of the North Bay offer sweeping panoramas.

89. Silverado Mine and Mount St. Helena Trail

Type: Dayhike
Difficulty: Moderate to difficult for children
Distance: 2 miles, round trip to Silverado Mine; 10 miles, round trip to peak
Hiking time: 1 hour to mine; 4 hours to peak
Elevation gain: 400 feet to mine; 2400 feet to peak
Hikable: Year-round
Map: USGS Detert Reservoir Topographic

To climb a peak, especially the tallest one around, is often a challenge that cannot be resisted by children. Mount St. Helena, which sits at the junction of Sonoma, Lake, and Napa counties, is the ultimate challenge for families in the North Bay. At 4343 feet, it is taller than either Mount Tamalpais in Marin County or Mount Diablo in the East Bay, but is not an impossible climb. On a clear day you can see from the Pacific Ocean to the Sierra Nevada, and all of the San Francisco Bay

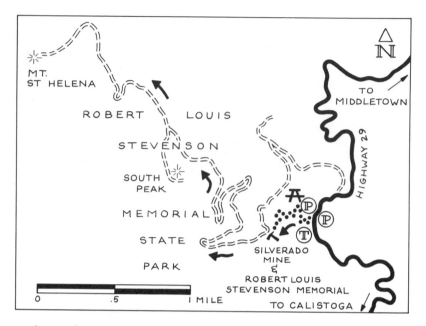

region to the south. Bring a map and binoculars so you can pick out all the many landmarks that are visible.

Although there is still some speculation about how Mount St. Helena was formed, there is near universal agreement among geologists that it was not part of a cone or dome. Instead, most now feel that the peak and the rugged volcanic Palisades to the southeast were formed through folding and uplifting that left vents through which lava flowed to the surface. The rock here is much older than the volcanic region near Clear Lake just to the north, and the activities do not seem to have much connection with each other.

Take CA-29 north from Calistoga for 7 very winding and slow miles to the parking lot of Robert Louis Stevenson Memorial State Park. Use the parking lot on the left side of the road for the easiest access to the trail, which leads west from the rear of the parking area.

Twelve wooden steps lead out of the parking area to the trail. After about 100 yards, you will come to a flat spot with picnic tables that was once the site of the Toll House Hotel. The old stage road descends from the flat to the north and the signs for the trail to the summit are on the west side of the flat.

The initial mile of trail leads through a dense mixed forest with various oak, bay, madrone, and fir. Various bushes compete for light and food underneath the heavy canopy of the large trees that cover the steep slopes, and wildflowers thrive there in the late spring.

The first switchback in this steep climb begins less than 200 yards from the beginning of the trail, and there are many more in the first 0.5 mile. The extensive erosion between the switchbacks is an excellent example of why hikers should not cut across switchbacks.

After 0.5 mile, the forest thins out somewhat and views of the rugged slopes are revealed. Manzanita and knobcone pine begin to appear along the trail, as well as rocky outcrops.

The trail reaches the Robert Louis Stevenson Memorial at 0.75 mile. A plaque sits at the site of the bunkhouse where Stevenson and his wife honeymooned in the summer of 1880. Although little sunlight reaches the spot today, Stevenson's writings indicate that the clearing was larger a century ago. From the plaque a trail leads up to the old Silverado Mine, which was operating when Stevenson lived there.

For those who do not want to attempt the long and arduous climb to the peak, this is a good turnaround spot. For climbers going to the top, the trail climbs steeply out of the flat to a ridge that offers good views to Lake County in the north.

The trail climbs rapidly to a gravel fire road at about 1 mile. From here it is just over 4 miles to North Peak (the main peak), and 3 miles to South Peak. The hike changes from a narrow, steep trail to a wide, easy fire road, as the intimacy offered by the heavy canopy of the forest below gives way to open views and glaring exposure to midday sun. Views of all of Napa Valley open up within 100 yards, and the road climbs through chaparral toward the south of the peak.

The first big switchbacks on this section of the trail are at 1.5 miles, and a small stand of digger (or gray) pine can be seen above the trail. A large rock outcropping is also seen here.

The trail continues a steady, easy climb to a big switchback at 2.25 miles, where Snow Mountain, a 7056-foot peak in Mendocino County, comes into view to the northwest.

The trail passes under some power lines around 3 miles and continues its easy climb through chaparral and rock outcroppings. South Peak Trail spur leads off to the left at 3.5 miles. This short spur (about 0.25 mile) leads to the 4003-foot summit of South Peak, and is a good turnaround point if your youngsters have overestimated their ability (or desire!) to trek to the top. With this spur, you can at least claim to have climbed a peak, even if not the tallest one around.

The trail to North Peak continues straight ahead with several ups and downs, and at about 4 miles the trail climbs to the main ridge leading to the top. The roughest part of the climb comes between here and 4.5 miles, when the climb again eases.

Fir and nutmeg are the dominant trees here, but sugar pine soon appear beside the trail. The California nutmeg is a close relative of the yew found in the Pacific Northwest, and is not related to the spice nutmeg as far as I can determine. It is a small evergreen that has glossy dark green leaves that look something like redwood leaves. They are easily distinguished, however, by the sharp points on the end of the leaves that are very noticeable when you attempt to push through them.

The trail passes back under the power lines, and through a forest of large fir and sugar pines to the final climb to the peak. Just past 4.5 miles, the trail leaves the forest. A generator for a television station transmitter makes an awful noise as you pass it on your right, and you reach the top of the peak at just under 5 miles.

The noise from the generator fades somewhat as you walk down the north face of the peak, and you can enjoy the view of miles of Coast Range. On a clear day you can see Mount Shasta 200 miles to the northeast, Lassen Peak to its right, and even the high country of Yosemite to the southeast.

Retrace your route back to the parking area.

Several reminders on this trip. It gets very hot along the open trail in the summer, so always carry plenty of water. Also, the weather is never completely predictable on the peak, so be prepared for both hot and cold by dressing in layers and carrying a few more overgarments than you think you might need at the lower elevations.

---

90. Redwood/Ritchey Canyon Trail

Type: Dayhike
Difficulty: Difficult for children
Distance: 4.5 miles, round trip
Hiking time: 2 hours
Elevation gain: 650 feet
Hikable: Year-round
Map: USGS Calistoga Topographic

This 1900-acre state park is one of only two developed state parks in Napa County (Robert Louis Stevenson Memorial State Park is undeveloped except for the trail to Silverado Mine and Mount St. Helena), and it offers visitors camping and picnicking as well as about 10 miles of hiking trails. The park was operated as a private campground and resort known as Paradise Park for many years before the state acquired the property and developed it as Bothe–Napa Valley State Park in 1960. It and the adjoining Bale Grist Mill State Historic Park sit in the midst of the vineyards of the upper Napa Valley. The farther away from the campsites and the day activities of the park, the more likely you are to see some of the wildlife of Bothe–Napa Valley State Park. Raccoons, gray

The majesty of towering redwoods is almost overwhelming.

squirrels, deer, fox, bobcats, and coyote all live in the canyons of Ritchey Creek, along with six different kinds of woodpeckers, including the spectacular pileated woodpecker.

Take CA-29 north of St. Helena for 4 miles. Turn left into the entrance to the park.

Ritchey Canyon Trail begins at the horse trailer parking lot and heads west up Ritchey Creek. It skirts the south side of the creek opposite the Ritchey Creek Campground. Just beyond 0.25 mile, the Ritchey Canyon Trail forks off to the right and crosses the creek. The Redwood Trail forks to the left. Take this fork along the creek bank and through a forest of large redwood and fir. The trail passes a drinking fountain and climbs along the creek, and after about 100 yards passes by a small waterfall that cascades over a concrete dam.

Just past the large buckeye tree on the right the trail forks. The right fork leads to the campground and the Ritchey Canyon Trail on the other side of the creek. Continue straight on Redwood Trail as it climbs gently to the southwest. As the trail levels out, there is a large fir on the left that has large *conks*, a mushroom-like parasite that eats the tree from inside.

Around 0.5 mile, the redwoods thin out, and at the top of the hill at 0.75 mile all trees give way to open grassland and chaparral. As you

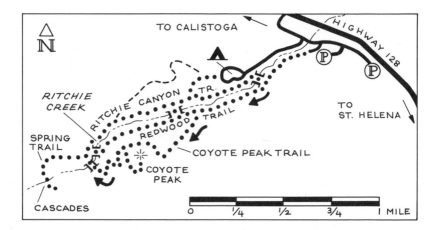

reach the top of the next hill, the Coyote Peak Trail leads off to the left. (If you wish to cut the hike short, continue on the Redwood Trail about 100 yards past the junction with the Coyote Peak Trail, cross over the creek on a footbridge, and return to the trailhead along the Ritchey Canyon Trail on the opposite side of the creek.)

The Coyote Peak Trail leads through most of the plant communities of the park as it climbs from 500 to 1170 feet at the top of Coyote Peak. The north slope is forested with a heavy undercover. The trail also offers views up Ritchey Canyon as it follows the contour of Coyote Peak.

At 1.25 miles, take the spur trail to the peak that leads off to the left. The peak is a good place to rest and enjoy the views before heading back down.

Return to the Coyote Peak Trail and turn left to head down the steep slopes through chaparral on the more exposed west slope before joining with the Spring Trail at 1.75 miles. Coyote Peak, Redwood, Spring, and Ritchey Canyon trails all join just past Ritchey Creek, where you take a footbridge across the creek. During a wet winter this may be impassable. If so, follow the creek downhill for several hundred feet to the Redwood Trail and return to the parking area.

Just over the creek at the junction of the Coyote, Redwood, Spring, and Ritchey Canyon trails take a left turn and head up the canyon. The trail climbs up the canyon away from the creek until you are about 100 feet above it. The trail levels and drops back down to the creek at 1.75 miles.

You can ford the creek here to reach a side stream cascading down over moss-covered rocks. This is an excellent site for a rest stop and lunch before you head back down the trail. For a slightly different look at the creek you can return by the Ritchey Canyon Trail on the north side of the creek.

Index

What? Who, me?

BILL McMILLON has been exploring the outdoors since his boyhood days. A teacher, counselor, and administrator in California and Arizona for seventeen years, Bill now writes full time, and is the author of *California's Underwater State Parks—A Diver's Guide; Volunteer Vacations;* and *Nature Nearby,* among others. He credits his 9-year-old son Kevin, an enthusiastic hiking companion, as co-author of this book.

The MOUNTAINEERS, founded in 1906, is a non-profit outdoor activity and conservation club, whose mission is "to explore, study, preserve and enjoy the natural beauty of the outdoors...." Based in Seattle, Washington, the club is now the third largest such organization in the United States, with 15,000 members and five branches throughout Washington State.

The Mountaineers sponsors both classes and year-round outdoor activities in the Pacific Northwest, which include hiking, mountain climbing, ski-touring, snowshoeing, bicycling, camping, kayaking and canoeing, nature study, sailing, and adventure travel. The club's conservation division supports environmental causes through educational activities, sponsoring legislation, and presenting informational programs. All club activities are led by skilled, experienced volunteers, who are dedicated to promoting safe and responsible enjoyment and preservation of the outdoors.

The Mountaineers Books, an active, non-profit publishing program of the club, produces guidebooks, instructional texts, historical works, natural history guides, and works on environmental conservation. All books produced by The Mountaineers are aimed at fulfilling the club's mission.

If you would like to participate in these organized outdoor activities or the club's programs, consider a membership in The Mountaineers. For information and an application, write or call The Mountaineers, Club Headquarters, 300 Third Avenue West, Seattle, Washington 98119; (206) 284-6310.